MY KOSOVO EXPERIENCE

MY KOSOVO EXPERIENCE

Perspectives on Europe's Newest State

Edited by

FATON TONY BISLIMI

Contributors:

Masayuki Kishimoto

Laura Lussier

Gordon MacKinnon

The Balkans
FREE PRESS
International Publishing House

Edmonton | Houston

ISBN-13: 978-0988160828
ISBN-10: 098816082X
Printed in Canada and the United States of America

This book is based on contributions by participants of the
Balkans Peace Program – Summer 2012. This program was
implemented and administered by the Bislimi Group Foundation
and took place in late May and June 2012 in Kosovo.

Proceeds from this book go to support the Balkans Peace
Program of the Bislimi Group Foundation.

For more information on the program or the foundation, please
visit: www.bislimi.org

MY KOSOVO EXPERIENCE

TABLE OF CONTENTS

Acknowledgements   1

Introduction   3

Chapter 1   9
The US and EU Roles in Creating Europe's Newest
State—Kosovo and International State Crafting
by Faton Tony Bislimi

Chapter 2   51
Transforming Balkanized Cultures: Seeing Schools
as Advocates for Change
by Gordon MacKinnon

Chapter 3   83
Kosovo—Where Optimism and Hope Never Die
by Laura Lussier

Chapter 4   125
Kosovo—An Unforgettable Experience
by Masayuki Kishimoto

Quotes from the Balkans Peace Program 2012   165

About Contributors   169

ACKNOWLEDGEMENTS

I WOULD LIKE TO THANK all of the participants of the Balkans Peace Program – Summer 2012 who travelled from half the way around the world to be part of this program: Jessica Alexander, Masa Kishimoto, Andrew Lawrance, Laura Lussier, and Gordie MacKinnon. I would like to also thank the Kosovar host brothers and sisters and their families who made sure the foreign students on the program felt at home: Alban Hyseni, Behar Ibishi, Adelina Jerliu, Leonard Miftaraj, Armend Shala, Elvira Zenuni, and Albert Xhaqkaj.

Special thanks go to Halit Bislimi and to all of my foundation's volunteers for their help in making this program a true success. Thanks go also to Milot Shkodra and the Gjilani University College, Halil Korcaj, and Xhevat Latifi for all their support.

My most heartfelt gratitude and appreciation are extended to the President of Kosovo H.E. Atifete Jahjaga, Deputy Ministers Hajdin Abazi, Ibrahim Gashi, and Izmi Zeka, Mayor of Gjilan Qemajl Mustafa, and other political and government officials who met with our BPP participants.

Special thanks go to Judy Hinkhouse for her tireless and excellent work in copyediting this book.

Lastly, I would have never been able to put this program as well as this book together without the endless love and support from my beautiful wife, Nora, and my princess daughter, Fiona.

Faton Tony Bislimi
Editor

INTRODUCTION

WHEN I first thought about establishing a summer program for foreign students in Kosovo, I had several key ideas in mind. I wanted the program to be academic. I also wanted the program to be fun. The program also had to be culturally immersing. It had to include a tour of the neighbouring countries.

As I tried to put all of these requirements together into one program, I realized that while it may seem impossible, it can actually be done. So, I made sure the Balkans Peace Program would consist of three key components—academic, cultural, and educational.

To satisfy the first requirement—academic—students on the program would be offered an intensive (seminar-like) course on the theme of the program, namely international development, peacekeeping, peace-building, post-conflict reconstruction, state-building, etc.

To satisfy the second component—cultural immersion—I decided that the foreign students participating in the program would stay with local host families who would have a son or daughter of similar age and who speaks English to become the official host brother or host sister of the foreign student. Moreover, to diversify the class, I opened up the program (its academic component, the course) to local students with an interest in the topic and with good English proficiency.

To satisfy the third component—educational—the program would provide the students with a tour of not only Kosovo's key historic and natural attractions but also of some of the most renowned places of historic or touristic value in Kosovo's neighbouring countries of Montenegro, Albania, and Macedonia.

The Balkans Peace Program 2012 marked the beginning of this flagship program of my foundation, the Bislimi Group Foundation.

As this book comes to light, the second cohort (class of 2013) of the Balkans Peace Program is making their final preparations to head to Kosovo. Why Kosovo? Well, there are several characteristics that make Kosovo a unique place. Putting aside the very obvious reasons—such as the fact that Kosovo is my home country and I share an indescribable connection with it—Kosovo is unique both in terms of its history and the present developments. Despite being a rather small country in Europe, Kosovo is of international relevance, especially politically. During the Kosovo War of 1998-99, the world was bitterly divided on the issue of whether a military intervention by NATO was legal and just, as NATO embarked on a 78-day bombing campaign against Serbia in an effort to stop ethnic cleansing and mass murders against innocent ethnic Albanians in Kosovo.

Once the war ended, Kosovo was put under international administration headed by the UN. The UN Mission in Kosovo (UNMIK) became the legislative, administrative, and executive body governing Kosovo on the basis of the UN Security Council Resolution 1244 of June 1999. This was the first time in the history of the UN that the UN had undertaken such an ambitious role—to govern a territory.

From an international relations perspective, NATO's intervention to save Kosovo and UN's taking over to govern it, for instance, show the uniqueness of Kosovo.

Moreover, Kosovo is unique also in the way it has undertaken its state-building process. I will talk in greater details about this in Chapter 1.

Kosovo is the only country in Europe in which over half of the population is under the age of twenty-five. Kosovo is, unfortunately, the poorest country in Europe as well.

On February 17, 2008, Kosovo declared its independence and thus far it has been recognized by close to 100 nations around the world. Yet, Kosovo is not a member of the UN and, as a result, cannot participate in many international sports events as a nation.

Over 90% of Kosovo's population is made up by ethnic Albanians, with about 8% being ethnic Serbs and the rest being of Roma, Ashkali, Egyptian, Turkish and other ethnic origins. Yet, Kosovo is defined as a multi-ethnic state and provides its minority communities with some of the most advanced rights, constitutionally guaranteed.

Kosovo is a great place to be if you are interested in studying post-conflict societies, international development or related topics. It is located in Europe; it is safe; and it is developing.

So, it provides the right environment for students with an interest in such topics as aforementioned. And, I am certain that the Balkans Peace Program 2012 participants enjoyed their Kosovo experience.

In this book, apart from the first chapter which is a way of giving the reader a better understanding of Kosovo's state-building process from a theoretical perspective (in which I evaluate the roles that the US and EU have played in this process), the rest of the chapters are original contributions by the BPP 2012 participants.

I am very thankful to Masayuki Kishimoto (originally from Japan, studying at Mount Saint Vincent University in Halifax, NS, Canada), Laura Lussier (studying at McGill University in Montreal, Quebec, Canada), and Gordon MacKinnon (who was finishing up his Med at Mount Saint Vincent University in Halifax, NS, Canada when he joined the program) for sharing their Kosovo experience with us. As you will see, they all came out of the program with a different take. They all have different perspectives on many things and issues. While their stories are personal, they tell the story of Kosovo. As diverse as these stories' perspectives are, so is the actual life in Kosovo. Problems and issues coexist with hope, optimism, and good things.

Faton Tony Bislimi

22 March 2013

CHAPTER 1

The US and EU Roles in Creating Europe's Newest State: Kosovo and International State Crafting *

Faton Tony Bislimi

* This chapter has been published in Finn Laursen (Ed.) *The EU, Security and Transatlantic Relations*, Brussels/New York: PIE Peter Lang, 2012. ISBN978-90-5201-889-8.

THE INTERNATIONAL military intervention by NATO against Serbia in the Kosovo War of 1998-99 marked NATO's first ever war and its first ever intervention without a Security Council approval. This intervention, however, enabled the UN to take over, for the first time in its history, the administration of a territory. Supported heavily by both the US and the EU, the international intervention in Kosovo provides an important instance of state crafting under the auspices of the international community. Indeed, the two key players in post-war Kosovo have been the US and the EU. For almost ten years, while Kosovo was under the UN administration, the US and the EU were unable to find a cohesive and mutually agreeable solution to Kosovo's political status. Even in post-independence Kosovo, both the US and EU remain key players. This chapter, therefore, looks at the differences and similarities in the US and EU responses and their approaches to the Kosovo problem since the beginning of the Kosovo War in 1998. This is not to say, however, that the Kosovo problem did not exist before the war. I look at three key phases of the process that created the newest state in Europe, the Republic of Kosovo, in which both the US and EU were important actors. Given that the end result of this joint US-EU exercise in the Balkans was the creation of an independent state, I use two key state-building theories to explain the US and EU approaches – deconstruction and cooption. The three phases I identify are the war period, the period of UN rule over Kosovo, and the post-independence period. Based on the US and EU's intensity of involvement in Kosovo in these three particular phases, I determine their respective roles as supporting, participating, or leading actors.

1. Introduction

As NATO was getting ready to celebrate its fiftieth anniversary in 1999, it was faced with an enormous challenge in the very backyard of the European Union. The war in Kosovo was escalating and so was the refugee crisis with over one million Kosovars having been forced into its neighbouring countries due to ethnic cleansing committed by the Serbian regime of the time. With the international community's diplomatic efforts to end the war having ultimately failed after the Kosovar Albanian delegation signed the Rambouillet Agreement, but the Serbs did not, NATO's credibility was put in line given the use of force threat it had issued at the beginning of the Rambouillet conference.

Without a clear UN Security Council mandate, but dedicated to protect innocent civilians in Kosovo, under the leadership of the US, NATO marked its first ever war when it started a 78-day bombing campaign against Serbia. To date, NATO remains present in Kosovo and so does the EU. They have both played an important role in shaping Kosovo's post-war future.

Indeed, the two key players in post-war Kosovo have been the US and the EU. For almost ten years, while Kosovo was under the UN administration, the US and the EU were unable to find a cohesive and mutually agreeable solution to Kosovo's political status. It was the American dedication to end the status-quo in Kosovo that was also supported by the EU that finally brought about Kosovo's independence. Even in post-independence Kosovo, both the US and EU remain key players. A small nation in the backyard of the EU, Kosovo has turned to be an important issue for the foreign and security policies of both the US and EU.

This chapter, therefore, looks at the differences and similarities in the US and EU responses and their approaches to the Kosovo problem since the beginning of the Kosovo War in 1998. This is not to say, however, that the Kosovo problem did not exist before the war. The Kosovo problem is perhaps the oldest problem in the turbulent history of the Balkans. So, I look at three key phases of the process that created the newest state in Europe, the Republic of Kosovo, in which both the US and EU were important actors. Given that the end result of this joint US-EU exercise in the Balkans was the creation of an independent state, I use two key state-building theories to explain the US and EU approaches – deconstruction and cooption. The three phases

I identify are the war period, the period of UN rule over Kosovo, and the post-independence period. Based on the US and EU's intensity of involvement in Kosovo in these three particular phases, I determine their respective roles as supporting, participating, or leading actors.

The chapter does also briefly look at the approaches that the US and EU took as the Kosovo problem went from bad to worse in the 1980s and 1990s. Despite the fact that Kosovo was right in the backyard of the EU, during this time, the role of the EU was that of a distant monitor whereas that the US a close monitor.

The transatlantic relations between the US and EU have certainly been shaped by the Kosovo problem. But, these relations have also shaped the way in which the new state of Kosovo was crafted.

Finally, I will provide some concluding remarks that bring one key conclusion to light: as the US role in Kosovo decreased, the EU role increased. The process of international state crafting in the case of Kosovo seems to be a zero-sum game, in which what one actor loses the other gains, whether for good or bad, or whether willingly or not so willingly.

2. International State-Crafting in Kosovo and the US-EU Involvement

In what follows, the key three phases of the US and EU's involvement in Kosovo are elaborated, paying particular attention to the intensity or the leadership role that one or the other has taken. At each phase, as the role of the US decreases, one cannot but not how the EU role increases accordingly. From the involvement in the Kosovo War to the post-independence Kosovo, one can easily see how the roles of the US and the EU have shifted: the former has moved from a leading actor position to a participating actor, while the latter has moved in the exact opposite direction – from a participating actor to a leading actor position.

2.1. Kosovo War and NATO's Intervention: EU's Supportive Role

Before the Kosovo War of 1998-99, the international response to the growing crisis in Kosovo was sporadic, at best. A more sustained response, however, came from the United States. As early as 1986, when even within Kosovo there were only a handful of intellectual elites talking openly about the unfair treatment of Albanians within Yugoslavia, a couple of concurrent resolutions were introduced in the U.S. Congress to bring to the attention of the U.S. this problematic situation in Europe. H. CON. RES. 358 of 17 June 1986 condemning the repression of ethnic Albanians by the Government of the Socialist Federated Republic of Yugoslavia (SFRY) was introduced in the U.S. House of Representatives sponsored by U.S. Representative Joseph J. DioGuardi, concurrently with CON. RES. 150 expressing concern over the condition of ethnic Albanians living in the Socialist Federal Republic of Yugoslavia, which was introduced in the U.S. Senate sponsored by U.S. Senator Bob Dole (AACL: URL). The intensity of new resolutions being introduced in the U.S. Congress increased with time. Indeed, the Albanian-American diaspora played a key role in convincing the United States to take a firm stand in stopping ethnic cleansing and then brining about Kosovo's independence.

Contrary to the U.S., the European Union was more negligent about the situation in Kosovo, despite geo-strategic proximity of the latter to the EU. Indeed, despite the fact that former Yugoslavia was considered a problematic area that could threaten the values of the EU, the Union had neither the necessary "political will" nor "an underlying policy or appropriate mechanisms" to successfully get involved in the escalating crisis in former Yugoslavia (Muguruza, 2003). More specifically, until 6 April 1996 Kosovo was not even mentioned in any EU or EC documents. It is in the 'Declaration of Recognition by EU Member States of the Federal Republic of Yugoslavia (FRY),' which called for a larger autonomy for Kosovo within FRY of that date that Kosovo was referred to for the first time (Muguruza, 2003). By the time the EU was finally taking some interest in the unrest in Kosovo, the crisis there would approach its peak in just two years.

By 1998, the situation in Kosovo presented an inevitable descent into a full-fledged war. The brutal repression of the Serbian regime on the civilian Kosovo Albanian population increased in the spring of 1998 and the massacres of February-March of that year against ethnic Albanians strengthened the commitment of international community to seriously deal with Kosovo. In many ways, the brutality in Kosovo was a reminder to the international community of what had happened in Bosnia a few years earlier (Muguruza, 2003).

The Kosovo Liberation Army (KLA), which was created in December 1993 (Judah, 2008), was now seen as a key player in the Kosovo issue, despite the fact that the parallel state institutions of Kosovo remained committed to a peaceful resolution. KLA was funded and armed mainly by the Kosovo Albanian diaspora in Western Europe and the United States (Perritt, 2008; Sullivan, 2007).

A series of UN Security Council Resolutions, European Parliament Resolutions, EU joint actions, and common decisions, did not stop Milosevic from continuing his ethnic cleansing in Kosovo. Given the experience of the war in Bosnia and Croatia, it was generally accepted among international decision-making circles that Milosevic only understands the use of force (Reveron, 2002; Clark, 2002).

The international community, mainly under the auspices of the Contact Group for Kosovo (consisting of Britain, France, Germany, Italy, Russia, the U.S., and representatives of the European Union Presidency and the European Commission) worked intensively to bring a peaceful resolution to the Kosovo war. Partly as result of diplomacy and mainly due to NATO's threat to intervene militarily, Serbia accepted an OSCE (Organization for Security and Cooperation in Europe) peace mission, the Kosovo Verification Mission, to enter Kosovo in October 1998 (McKinnon, 2008; Hosmer, 2001).

At the same time, the Contact Group, this time greatly supported by the European Union as well, organized the Rambouillet Conference which aimed at bringing an end to the war in Kosovo. This was perhaps the last diplomatic attempt to resolve the crisis – especially after the OSCE Kosovo Verification Mission documented the massacre of 45 ethnic Albanian civilians by the Serbian forces on January 15, 1999. The Kosovo delegation at Rambouillet included representatives from the peaceful movement and KLA. To back up the diplomatic action of the Contact Group, NATO had issued a bombing warning for the non-complying party. The Rambouillet Conference concluded in diplomatic dismay when only the Kosovo Albanian delegation, despite the fact that the

Rambouillet Agreement would not grant Kosovo independence immediately, accepted the agreement while the Serbian/FRY delegation rejected it. The Serbian rejection of the internationally brokered peace agreement at Rambouillet marked the immediate start of NATO's activation order for airstrikes against FRY, which started on March 24, 1999 (Hosmer, 2001).

The 78-day NATO bombing campaign against Serbian targets throughout Kosovo and FRY ended with the Kumanovo Technical-Military Agreement between NATO and FRY, which gave way to the UN-mandated KFOR (Kosovo Force), a NATO-led military presence, to enter Kosovo in June 1999 while facilitating an immediate and complete withdrawal of all Serbian troops from Kosovo (Clark, 2002). NATO's mission in Kosovo mainly revolved around security and peacekeeping – providing a secure and peaceful place for all, protecting Kosovo's borders, and ensuring the demilitarization of the KLA (Clark, 2002).

With KFOR on the ground and the war over, a new era started in Kosovo. KFOR's mandate as a peacekeeper in Kosovo represents, perhaps, one of the most successful international peacekeeping operations involving NATO. In efforts to stimulate modern state-building and development, "well-meaning developed countries" have intervened in post-conflict and failed state situations in many ways, including "military occupation," but often such interventions have "actually made things worse"

(Fukuyama, 2004). If NATO's intervention in Kosovo is viewed as a military occupation, however, it is a successful one, despite Fukuyama's scepticism. Indeed, in the eyes of Kosovars, KFOR has been continuously ranked as the international institution enjoying the highest public satisfaction with an average satisfaction level of over 83% between November 2002 and April 2009 (UNDP, 2009).

Beyond its security mandate, however, KFOR has become also a social facilitator and reconciliatory actor between Kosovo Serbs and Albanians. It has also played an essential role in transforming the KLA into the Kosovo Protection Corps (KPC) after the war and it is now also charged with training and helping build the capacities of the Kosovo Security Force (KSF) in the post-independent Kosovo. Supporting community projects – such as building bridges, roads, schools, etc – has also become an important task of KFOR since its deployment to Kosovo in light of the weaknesses of other institutions to do so (KFOR: URL). What KFOR has been doing in Kosovo seems to be in line with a state-building process of peacekeepers that Fearon and Laitin (2004) define as a need for peacekeepers to "foster state-building if there is to be any hope for exist without a return to considerable violence." Other authors also assert that peace-building missions mean state-building (Paris, 2002; Barnett and Zuercher, 2008).

Furthermore, Dobbins et al. (2007) distinguish between two approaches to state-building: cooption and deconstruction. Cooption tries to work within existing institutions and is the approach mostly used by the UN. Deconstruction, which is mainly associated with the U.S. interventions, involves a process by which certain groups or existing state apparatus in the target society are disempowered while other groups within that society are empowered (Dobbins et al, 2007). The case of Kosovo, given NATO's military intervention and the post-war UN administration, provides an example of both these approaches being used.

NATO's U.S.-led intervention in Kosovo certainly disempowered all existing Serbian institutions. It simply got rid of all Serbian political and military instalments from Kosovo, and in due course empowered the post-war Kosovo institutions, now in the hands of the other groups in Kosovo, namely the Kosovo ethnic Albanians. This seems fully in line with the deconstruction approach to state-building. On the other hand, as we will see in the next section, the UN Mission in Kosovo (UNMIK) used a cooption approach to state-building in Kosovo.

Therefore, in light of the above, NATO's intervention in Kosovo presents the first phase of active US and EU involvement in international state-crafting in Kosovo, especially in terms of a deconstruction approach to state-building.

2.2. *Kosovo's UN Administration: EU's Active Participation*

UN Security Council Resolution 1244 of 10 June 1999 gave birth to what became known as UNMIK – the United Nations Interim Administration Mission in Kosovo. UNMIK was mandated by the UN Security Council to administer Kosovo until its final political status would be resolved. The resolution stipulated no duration for the mission. Once NATO troops entered Kosovo in June 1999 and consequently UNMIK deployed, within weeks, some 850,000 Kosovo refugees returned to their homes, in what can be regarded as the fastest and largest refugee return in recent history (Hysa, 2004).

UNMIK initially was organized into four major pillars. The first pillar was that of civil administration, the second was that of the judiciary (including the UN police), the third was in charge of institution building and elections (entrusted to the OSCE) and the fourth was the reconstruction and economic development pillar (a responsibility entrusted to the European Union). Post-independence, the role of UNMIK has been significantly reduced. As of June 2008, the UNMIK structure comprised the Democratization and Institution Building pillar under the auspices of OSCE (UNMIK, 2008).

Despite its unprecedented sweeping mandate to provide Kosovo with a "transitional administration while establishing and overseeing the development of provisional democratic self-governing institutions to ensure conditions for a peaceful and normal life for all inhabitants in Kosovo," (UNMIK, 2008) UNMIK itself was not democratic. As Chesterman (2004) notes, a 2003 report of the Ombudsperson in Kosovo clearly stated that "UNMIK is not structured according to democratic principles, does not function in accordance with the rule of law, and does not respect important international human rights norms. The people of Kosovo are therefore deprived of protection of their basic rights and freedoms three years after the end of the conflict by the very entity set up to guarantee them."

Nevertheless, UNMIK seemed to have understood immediately that without involvement of the local political leadership, its mission was next to impossible. Initially, UNMIK established a Joint Administrative Council (JAC), which was a government-like body, and the Kosovo Transitional Council (KTC), which was a legislature-like body. Yet, only UNMIK had the authority to decide any matters related to Kosovo (Hysa, 2004). The establishment of the Provisional Institutions of Self-Government (PISG) in Kosovo came after the first free and democratic elections were organized – locally in 2000 and nationally in 2001. With time, UNMIK transferred a series of competences to the PISG (UNMIK, 2008). Involvement of local political forces in the process of administering Kosovo since the beginning of the work of UNMIK presents a good example of facilitating "local ownership" which Narten (2006) argues is an essential part of successful state-building.

As the role of UNMIK started to fade away, the role of the EU increased in Kosovo, especially when negotiations on the final status of Kosovo started in late 2005. For the EU, Kosovo presented both a challenge and an opportunity in terms of its international crisis involvement.

The involvement of the international community in the Kosovo war and the post-war administration of Kosovo, found the EU unprepared to deal with such crisis. Kosovo served a precursor to the EU's commitment for a credible European security strategy, which resulted in the European Security and Defence Policy (ESDP). The EU security and defence policy was tasked to the Western European Union (WEU), but its capability was never fully operationalized in practice (Latawski and Smith, 2003). And, if WEU security and defence policies were to have any impact, they were to meet three key conditions, as defined by Bretherton and Vogler (2006): presence, opportunity and capability. Since WEU did not have capability, EU turned to ESDP given an important change in British policy in regards to the EU having its own capability in the area of defence and security policy that took place at the Saint-Malo meeting in 1998, in light of the violent events in Former Yugoslavia (Bretherton and Vogler, 2006).

So as the negotiations for the final status determination continued, Kosovars continuously grew tired of UNMIK's presence. In November 2002, the satisfaction of the Kosovo people with the UNMIK was as high as 65% while by December 2007, the satisfaction level dropped to only 27%. Apart from political reasons, mainly related to the prolongation of the final status determination, Kosovo under UNMIK was not progressing in terms of economic development either. Unemployment and poverty remained among key problems that Kosovars were faced with (UNDP, 2008).

The role of UNMIK finally became completely redundant when Kosovo declared independence on February 17, 2008, and the EU took over major tasks in post-independence Kosovo as we shall see in the next section.

But, despite its difficulties and perhaps sometimes undemocratic practices, UNMIK presents the second phase of the EU and US involvement in international state-crafting in Kosovo. In terms of Dobbins et al (2007), UNMIK presents the case of cooption approach to state-building in Kosovo. UNMIK, which has always kept a representative office in Belgrade, has always recognized the importance of Belgrade over Kosovo issues. Despite the non-existing Serbian regime establishments in post-war Kosovo itself, UNMIK nevertheless continued to work with Belgrade in all areas regarding socio-political and economic issues in Kosovo. This indicates that the cooption approach to state-building was also used in the case of Kosovo.

The work of UNMIK, furthermore, represents the involvement of international community in state-building.

UNMIK, as a UN-mandated mission, was practically a multilateral institution charged with building institutions of self-government in Kosovo. As such it also represents a good example of what Fearon and Laitin (2004) refer to as multilateral state-building "under the banner of neo-trusteeship."

Given its executive and legislative mandate over Kosovo, UNMIK (initially on its own and since 2001 in consultation with the PISG) brought about a series of regulations to Kosovo, signed international treaties on behalf of Kosovo, among other things. It is in this way that Kosovo under UNMIK became a player on the international stage. For instance, in 2006 Kosovo entered the Central European Free Trade Agreement (CEFTA), became a participant of the European Stabilization and Association Process (SAP), and approved the European Partnership Action Plan (EPAP). This international engagement of Kosovo under UNMIK is in line with Paris' (2002) assertion that peace-building missions serve as mechanisms for globalization of values and institutions.

It should also be noted that the structure and role of UNMIK is fully in line with tasks that Dobbins et al (2007) ascribe to nation-building such as: security - rule of law; humanitarian relief – return of refugees; governance – public administration; economic stabilisation; democratization – elections; and development – economic growth. In UNMIK terms, these tasks translate as follows: security – UN police and judiciary; humanitarian relief – facilitating the return of refugees to Kosovo; governance – Pillar One tasked with Civil Administration; economic stabilisation – facilitating a safe business environment and establishing Euro as the official currency in Kosovo; democratization – Pillar Three tasked with organizing elections and promoting democracy under the leadership of OSCE; and development – Pillar Four under the EU, promoting economic growth through facilitation of Kosovo's presence in CEFTA and other economic initiatives.

2.3. *The Ahtisaari Plan for Supervised Independence: EU's Front Seat Role through EULEX and ICO[1]*

With the appointment of Martti Ahtisaari, a former Finnish president, as UN Special Envoy for the Kosovo final status talks between Prishtina and Belgrade in November 2005, a fourteen-month long negotiations process to find a political compromise for Kosovo's final status took place in Vienna. Yet, Prishtina and Belgrade could not come to an agreement. As a result, in March 2007, Ahtisaari submitted to the UN Secretary-General a Comprehensive Proposal for the Settlement of the Kosovo Final Status. With his support, on 26 March 2007, Secretary-General forwarded the document to the UN Security

---

[1] The ICO's mandate in Kosovo came to an end in September 2012 (after this paper was originally written), but the EUSR office continues to operate to date.

Council for consideration. It was expected that the UN Security Council, in light of the Ahtisaari Plan, would reach a new resolution superseding UNSC Resolution 1244, and mandating a new international presence in Kosovo to help implement the Plan (ICG, 2007).

The Ahtisaari Plan envisioned a multiethnic, independent Kosovo under international supervision. It gave Kosovo supervised independence – which would satisfy the objectives of the majority Kosovo Albanians, while it also gave a high degree of local autonomy to majority Serbian municipalities within Kosovo, including special links with Serbia through a decentralization process that was an integral part of the Plan. Moreover, the Plan called for major and substantial EU involvement in the fields of justice, rule of law, and customs and for an International Civilian Office (ICO) to ensure the full implementation of the plan. The chief of ICO, the International Civilian Representative (ICR) would still have executive powers and could intervene to override legislation or other decisions of the Kosovo authorities if they were deemed to be in violation of the letter or spirit of the Plan. The EU rule of law, justice, and customs mission would also have a rather limited executive mandate. KFOR's presence was deemed necessary to continue while the Kosovo Protection Corps would be dissolved and a new, modern but small military force called the Kosovo Security Force would be created under KFOR's guidance and direction.

The Plan also suggested that continuation of international administration in Kosovo was not sustainable (UNOSEK, 2007). Once the Ahtisaari Plan was introduced in the UN Security Council, a sharp divide ensued among Western powers on one side and Russia and China on the other. The U.S. and E.U. were fully in support of the Plan, but Russia firmly opposed it – claiming that without Serbia's consent, Kosovo cannot become independent as it would set a dangerous precedent for other separatist movements around the world and especially in Eurasia (Antonenko, 2007). On the other hand, the U.S. and E.U. saw Kosovo's independence as sui generis. In a statement to the UN Security Council, UK Ambassador Sawers said "the unique circumstances of the violent break-up of the former Yugoslavia and the unprecedented UN administration of Kosovo make this a sui generis case, which creates no wider precedent, as all EU member States today agreed" (UN News Centre, 2008).

As no progress was in near sight at the UN Security Council given Russia's threat to veto any new UN Security Council resolution giving way to Kosovo's independence, the Kosovo authorities, in close coordination with Washington and Brussels, unilaterally declared Kosovo an independent and sovereign state on February 17, 2008. Kosovo's Declaration of Independence, however, made specific mention of the Ahtisaari Plan and pledged that Kosovo would fully implement it (Assembly of Kosovo, 2008).

So without a new UN Security Council resolution, UNMIK's existence continued, despite the fact that its role as an all-powerful entity expired with Kosovo's declaration of independence. A new international presence, however, was established in post-independence Kosovo: the EU Rule of Law Mission (EULEX) and ICO, headed by the ICR/EU Special Representative (EUSR). At first glance, it may seem that indeed UNMIK was replaced by an EU Mission. But, there are substantial differences between the two.

Let's recall that EU was given a role within UNMIK as well – tasked with reconstruction (William, 2005), but that was not because of EU's political importance but rather because of UN's need for EU's economic and development resources necessary for the post-war Kosovo (King and Mason, 2006). EULEX, however, represents the most ambitious EU mission ever and the largest of all twenty-two ESDP missions to date (Pond, 2008). As opposed to UNMIK, EULEX does not have a civil administration mandate and it cannot adopt legislation or regulations on behalf of Kosovo. The EULEX mission statement stipulates that "EULEX is not in Kosovo to govern or rule." Its legal basis stems from the European Council Joint Action 2008/124/CFSP of 4 February 2008 (EULEX: URL). While EULEX does not enjoy a UN mandate, it deployed at the invitation of the Kosovo government (Pond, 2008). Despite the fact that EULEX is an EU mission, non-EU member states such as the U.S., Canada, Turkey, and Norway have also contributed police officers to it (EUSR, 2009).

The International Civilian Office, on the other hand, is headed by a double-mandated International Civilian Representative (ICR) / EU Special Representative (EUSR). The ICR/EUSR reports to the European Council and the International Steering Group (ISG) on Kosovo. The purpose of the ICO, however, is "international support for a European future" for Kosovo and its aims include "ensuring full implementation of the Kosovo's status settlement and supporting Kosovo's European integration." ICO strives to achieve its purpose and aims by "advising Kosovo's government and community leaders" (ICO: URL).

Even though both EULEX and ICO are relatively new in their presence in Kosovo, opinion polls indicate a favourable assessment of their roles by the Kosovo public. Approval ratings for EULEX, for instance, in the beginning of its mission in May 2008 were relatively low, only about 12%, while by April 2009, the approval ratings more than tripled to about 40%, which was slightly higher than approval ratings for either the Government or Assembly of Kosovo (UNDP, 2009).

Given the context and missions of both EULEX and ICO, it seems that Kosovo's way forward as an independent state, currently recognized by some 76 countries, is inseparably connected to its prospects of a European future. So, one challenge of state-building which refers to what kind of state is being built (Samuels and von Esiedel, 2004), in the case of Kosovo seems properly addressed. State-building in Kosovo, in light of Kosovo's aspiration for EU integration and international community's intention to help Kosovo in that direction, seems to be building a European state in Kosovo. Another question that remains open, however, is when will the EU be able to leave full sovereignty in the hands of Kosovars? Fearon and Laitin (2004) argue that perhaps embedded monitoring by international institutions may be a more appropriate aim of state-building process in the context of neo-trusteeship. And, it is likely that in the case of Kosovo, EU supervision either through EULEX, ICO or both, will continue until Kosovo's full integration into the EU, which is when, indeed EU monitoring would actually be "embedded" in Kosovo.

Given Kosovo's aspirations for a European future and the fact that democracy is at the core of EU values, a full-fledged and functioning democracy in Kosovo is required, among others, before Kosovo can join the EU. Whether Kosovo has come to meet this criterion yet remains to be seen as Kosovo conducts itself and its policies as an independent state from now on. But, democracy must be promoted and nourished even though Kosovo may not be a "well-functioning state" yet (Carothers, 2007).

Therefore, what we see in post-independence Kosovo is the third phase of the EU and US involvement in international state-crafting in Kosovo. It includes the declaration of independence, partial but significant international recognition, and an increased EU involvement through EULEX and ICO with objectives of bringing Kosovo to its European future. As an independent nation, by late June 2009, Kosovo became the 186th member of the IMF (IMF, 2009) and the newest member of the World Bank Group by joining "the IBRD, the International Development Association (IDA), the International Finance Corporation (IFC), the Multilateral Investment Guarantee Agency (MIGA), and the International Centre for Settlement of Investment Disputes (ICSID). With the admission of Kosovo, membership now stands at 186 countries for IBRD, 169 for IDA, 182 for IFC, 174 for MIGA, and 144 for ICSID" (World Bank, 2009). Kosovo's policy-makers and politicians do see Kosovo's membership in the IMF and the World Bank Group as a way forward to ensuring that more countries will recognize Kosovo and that "because the IMF is an international club, joining also is an important step on an arduous road to acceptance as a member of the international community" (Andrews and Davis, 2009)

The international involvement, especially that of the EU, in post-independence Kosovo seems to answer a challenging state-building question of what kind of state Kosovo is to be.

The answer to this question, however, does not conclude the state-building process in Kosovo. Indeed, the process may continue for many more years, especially in the fields of democracy promotion and sustainable development.

3. International Involvement in Shaping a New State's Institutions

The following two sections of the chapter provide a closer look at how the US and EU's involvement in international institutions and presences in Kosovo has shaped the creation of Kosovo's own state institutions and what the views of the people of Kosovo are vis-à-vis these international bodies operating in Kosovo in comparison to Kosovo's own government.

3.1. Puppet Political Institutions

When the first internationally organized, supervised, and recognized, free and fair local elections took place in post-war Kosovo in October 2000, representatives of the international community working in Kosovo – either for the UN or EU or NATO – were positively surprised with the high voter turnout of 79% (KAM, 2000). However, what we see right after the 2000 elections is a significant drop in voter turnout in only one year's time. The voter turnout in Kosovo's national elections of 2001 was not higher than 64% (CEC: URL)—down by some 15 percentage points from a year before. This negative trend of voter turnout has continued all the way to the latest national Kosovo elections of 2007 (54%) and local elections of 2009 (45%) (CEC: URL).

One major reason that may help us understand why the Kosovo electorate was seemingly losing its trust for the power of vote and thus turning away from one of the fundamental rights of democracy is related to the role of UNMIK in particular and the international presence in Kosovo in general.

According to UNMIK Regulation 1999/1, UNMIK became both the executive and legislative body of power in Kosovo. Despite the fact that UNMIK organized elections in Kosovo and established institutions of self-government, all powers rested with it and the Special Representative of the Secretary-General (head of UNMIK). Indeed, even the Constitutional Framework that gave rise to Kosovo's Provisional Institutions of Self-Government was formulated in a way that could exclusively be changed only by the SRSG and stipulated that all powers of the PISG were derived from the powers of the SRSG and always required his or her approval. No matter what the Kosovo elected institutions would say or decide, the SRSG could override it. So, going out to vote for political institutions that, expect for the name, did not bear much power seemed unimportant.

Furthermore, the proportional electoral system with one electoral district can be considered as another contributing factor to the decreasing voter turnout. Many think-tanks and civil society organizations have continuously pressured the international community and Kosovo's institutions to change the electoral system from a one-district system to a multi-district system (KDI, 2008). Just recently, political parties have also started to publicly speak in favour of a multi-district electoral system and call for necessary changes to the election laws (Frangu, 2010). It makes sense that Members of Parliament that would be directly elected by their own district electorate would have to be more responsible and accountable to their constituents as opposed to those elected through political parties based on a one-district electoral system.

Whether the political institutions of post-war Kosovo had any real power or not, people's satisfaction with their work seems to have decreased with voter turnout. According to UNDP's Kosovo Early Warning Report, one can see that from a record-high satisfaction level of some 70-80% in 2002, people's satisfaction with the work of either the Government of Kosovo or the Assembly of Kosovo continuously dropped on average all the way to 2007 (UNDP, 2009). Indeed, this decrease in people's satisfaction with the work of Kosovo's political institutions seems to be independent of the share of power that these institutions had vis-à-vis UNMIK.

For example, right at the time when UNMIK had handed over a larger share of power to Kosovo's political institutions as the negotiations for the final status were approaching their end (in 2006 and 2007), people's satisfaction with these institutions hits record-low levels. What this may indicate, however, is the inability of Kosovo's political institutions to perform to the expectations of the people when more power was given to them. And, this inability could have come from many years of full dependence on UNMIK and EU to run Kosovo in terms of political administration and economic reconstruction, respectively. While the international community tried to develop democratic political institutions in Kosovo, by way of keeping them fully dependent on UNMIK's executive mandate, it shot itself in the foot since it gave Kosovars no good reason to believe in these institutions. Data from a UNDP Kosovo Early Warning Report shows that from 2003 all the way 2008, on average, more Kosovars held UNMIK responsible for Kosovo's political situation than the Government of Kosovo and Kosovo's political parties (UNDP, 2009), with a couple of exemptions (during the second half of 2006 when negotiations for the final status were ending, and late 2007 when Kosovo was getting ready to declare its independence). Since July 2008 (months after the declaration of independence of 17 February 2008), more Kosovars have been holding the Government of Kosovo and its political parties, as opposed to UNMIK, responsible for Kosovo's political situation. This indicates that people will no longer tolerate their own political institutions to hide behind the international presence in Kosovo when it comes to political responsibility and accountability.

3.2. Independent, but Supervised Political Institutions

When Kosovo declared its independence on 17 February 2008, it made sure that the Declaration of Independence (Declaration of Independence of Kosovo, 2008) would itself recognize the Ahtisaari Plan as the basis for the foundations of the new state. One major component of the Ahtisaari Plan that affects Kosovo's statehood and state-building process is the supervision of independence by the EU.

As discussed in the previous two chapters, EU's role in Kosovo has significantly increased post-independence through EULEX and ICO. But, what do these international presences (EULEX and ICO) mean for Kosovo political development? Have Kosovo's political institutions become fully independent now? De jure and de facto no, since they still depend on EULEX for rule of law issues and still need ICO's approval for major financial decisions or constitutional changes (Constitution of Kosovo, 2008).

Despite the fact that both ICO and EULEX continuously make remarks about their supervisory and not executive role in Kosovo, Kosovars seem to perceive EULEX, for instance, as directly responsible for Kosovo's political situation. As can be seen from Figure 2, the portion of Kosovars that find EULEX responsible for Kosovo's political situation has continuously and significantly increased. What is more worrisome is the fact that between June and September 2009, the portion of Kosovars holding EULEX responsible for Kosovo's political situation has increased while the portion of Kosovars holding the Government of Kosovo responsible for Kosovo's political situation has decreased. If this trend were to continue, we could face a situation similar to that with UNMIK in the first six years of post-war Kosovo: Kosovars would see the EU presence as more responsible than Kosovo's own political institutions for the country's political situation.

If Kosovo slides back into holding the EU presence more responsible than its own political institutions about its political situation, Kosovo loses the battle of consolidating its own institutions of the new state. Kosovo's political institutions cannot be fully consolidated unless they are held fully responsible for the country political situation. Delaying the consolidation process of these institutions prolongs the state-building process of Kosovo. The EU supervision of Kosovo's independence cannot now serve as a curtain behind which Kosovo's institutions can hide and thus avoid being responsible and accountable to Kosovo's people.

In a process of democratic state-building, proper institution-building is essential. So far, however, in the case of Kosovo it seems that domestic political institutions have usually taken a second seat in the process of state-building – first during the UNMIK time when they were deemed provisional and non-executive, and now under EULEX and ICO when they sometimes choose to be on the second seat. Institution-building under international authority is neither easy nor short, because of the fact that domestic institutions do not have all the room they want for political and policymaking manoeuvres they want or need to make (Tansey, 2007).

Not only are Kosovo institutions legally obliged to respect ICO and EULEX decisions, but they also sometimes prefer to have important political decisions be made by ICO and EULEX even though they could make such decisions on their own. It seems as if the international presence knows better and thus should be allowed to make those decisions on behalf of Kosovo. But, there are no guarantees that the international presence knows better or always has the right and good motivations to make the correct decisions (Bain, 2007).

For example, Kosovo has its own Anti Corruption Agency, but it has never acted against much talked about corruption affairs within government ministries and other public institutions. On the other hand, EULEX used its executive mandate and carried out several search operations in an effort to shed some light over claims of corruption involving high-ranking government officials (Telegrafi, 2010). Another example would be the Government of Kosovo's decision to announce a political strategy for integration of Kosovo's north only when such strategy was approved by the ICO and a European Ambassador in Kosovo took the lead in supporting and monitoring its implementation (Koha Ditore, 2010). Both of these examples are indicators of Kosovo's political institutions' unwillingness to act as independent actors yet.

Besides the issue of institution-building, the issue of sovereignty comes up in the context of EU's supervision of Kosovo's independence. Sovereignty is not a precursor to statehood; rather it is one fundamental characteristic of the state and is defined as "plenary competence that states prima facie possess" (Crawford, 2006). In the case of Kosovo, sovereignty was "seized" (Van Roermund, 2002) by UNMIK and the SRSG given their executive, legislative and judiciary powers over the territory. Even post-independence, Kosovo still lives under partially seized sovereignty given the executive roles of ICO and EULEX in certain areas of power.

If sovereignty is a central characteristic of the state and Kosovo does not have full sovereignty yet (while it is under supervision by the EU), then it seems that Kosovo is somewhat of a partial state. This brings us to the question of whether state-building can work without full sovereignty. By the same token, we can also ask whether it is possible to have full sovereignty without completing the state-building process.

Consequently, we see that what we face is a 'catch 22' situation because it seems that Kosovo will not be able to get full sovereignty until it builds a fully functional and democratic state, while it cannot build such a state until its sovereignty belongs to none but Kosovo.

In a recent trip to Kosovo, however, the EU's High Representative for Foreign Affairs and Security Policy, Catherine Ashton, stated that "The European Union is completely united in the belief that Kosovo's future is within the European Union," despite the fact that five EU member states have not yet recognized Kosovo (B92, 2010). Kosovo's joining of the EU, thus, may be the only way out of the current "catch 22" situation. The issue of sovereignty becomes much less important when Kosovo gets closer to EU membership, while the state-building process could be well advanced by helping Kosovo fulfill of all the required criteria to become eligible for EU membership. Without the prospects of EU membership, the political development of Kosovo would at best stagnate or completely collapse in the worst case scenario.

4. Concluding Remarks

It is apparent that without the support and involvement of the US and the EU, Kosovo would have never come to where it is today. The international community's support for Kosovo – namely under the leadership of either the US or the EU – has been essential to creating a new, democratic, and functioning state in Europe. Yes, this new state faces many problems and challenges, but it also has some opportunities before itself to make succeed as a new democracy.

Despite many problems that the international presences in Kosovo has faced and have brought upon Kosovo, from a transatlantic relations point of view, the international involvement in state-crafting in the case of Kosovo shows one important element in the US-EU relations in regards to their roles in international crises or international involvements: their engagement in Kosovo was a zero-sum game – when one was in the leadership role, the other was in the supporting role and vice-versa.

Given that a picture is worth one thousand words, I hope that the following table helps us better understand the key conclusion that this chapter brings out.

EU and US Involvement in Kosovo

	Pre-War (before 1998)	During the War (1998-99)	After the War (1999-2008)	After Independence (after 2008)
E.U.	Distant Monitor	Supporting Actor	Participating Actor	Leading Actor
U.S.	Close Monitor	Leading Actor	Participating Actor	Supporting Actor

Because this chapter does not fully elaborate the US and EU's roles in the Kosovo problem before 1998, their roles are determined to be those of monitors, since neither the US, nor the EU were part of any international presence in Kosovo. The US, however, had an information office in Prishtina, something the EU did not have at all. Hence, their labels as distant monitor for the EU (i.e. no presence on the ground, no sustained policy debate over Kosovo) and close monitor for the US (i.e. continued Congress resolutions, Department of State reports, and presence on the ground through the US Information Office). And, because the US led NATO's intervention in Kosovo, its role was that of a leading actor, whereas the role of the EU was rather supportive, partly because most of the EU member states are also NATO member states and partly because the EU as such had no military capabilities at that time.

In the post-war period, namely the UNMIK time, both the US and the EU held participating actor positions: the chiefs of UNMIK would always be European while the deputy chiefs would always be American; the EU was in charge of economic reconstruction, while the US led the diplomatic efforts at the UN to break out of the status-quo. Both, however, were actively involved during this time, despite the fact that perhaps formally, the UN was in charge, and therefore in the driving seat.

Finally, in the post-independence period, we see a complete shift from the war period. Now, as opposed to then, the EU has the position of the leading actor (i.e. EULEX and ICO), while the US that of a supporting actor (i.e. supporting the ICO and KFOR).

References:

Albanian American Civic League (AACL). *Congressional Records.* Available from http://blog.aacl.com/congressional-record/

Andrews N. and B. Davis (2009). "Kosovo Wins Acceptance to IMF" *The Wall Street Journal*, pp. A10 [7 May 2009]

Antonenko, Oksana (2007). *Russia and the Deadlock over Kosovo*, Brussels: IFRI

Assembly of Kosovo (2008). *Declaration of Independence* [17 February 2008]. Available from http://www.assembly-kosova.org/?cid=2,128,1635

B92 News Agency (2010). "Ashton says Kosovo's future is in the EU." 20 February 2010. Available from: http://www.b92.net/eng/news/politics-article.php?yyyy=2010&mm=02&dd=20&nav_id=65320

Bain, W. (2007) "In Praise of Folly: International Administration and the Corruption of Humanity" in Hehir and Robinson (Eds) *State-Building: Theory and Practice*, Oxon: Routledge

Barnett, Michael Christoph Zuercher (2008). "The Peace-builder's Contract: How External State-building Reinforces Weak Statehood," in Roland Paris and Timothy Sisk (Eds.) *The Dilemmas of Statebuilding: Confronting the contradictions of postwar peace operations*, London: Routledge

Bretherton, Charlotte and John Vogler (2006). *The European Union as a Global Actor* (2nd edition), London: Routledge

Carothers, Thomas (2007). "How Democracies Emerge: The 'Sequencing' Fallacy", *Journal of Democracy*, 18 (1), pp. 12-27

CEC – Central Elections Commission. Available from: http://www.kqz-ks.org/SKQZ-WEB/al/zgjedhjetekosoves/zgjedhjetepergjitshme.html

Clark, Wesley K. (2002). *Waging Modern War: Bosnia, Kosovo and the Future of Conflict*, Cambridge, MA: PublicAffairs

Chesterman, Simon (2004). "Building Democracy through Benevolent Autocracy: Consultation and Accountability in UN Transitional Administrations" in Edward Newman and Roland Rich (Eds.) *The UN Role in Promoting Democracy: Between Ideals and Reality*, New York: United Nations University Press

Constitution of the Republic of Kosovo (2008)

Crawford, J. (2006). *The Creation of States in International Law.* Oxford: Clarendon Press

Dobbins, James, Seth G. Jones, Keith Crane, and Beth Cole DeGrasse (2007). *The Beginner's Guide to Nation-Building*, Santa Monica: RAND National Security Research Division

EU Rule of Law Mission, EULEX Kosovo. *What is EULEX?* Available from http://www.eulex-kosovo.eu/?id=2

EUSR in Kosovo (2009). *EULEX Kosovo Fact Sheet.* Available from http://www.eusrinkosovo.eu/pdf/090406%20EULEX%20FOC.pdf

Fearon, James D and David D. Laitin (2004). "Neo-trusteeship and the Problem of Weak States," *International Security*, 28 (4), pp. 5-43

Fukuyama, Francis (2004). "The Imperative of State-Building", *Journal of Democracy*, 15 (2), pp. 17-31

Hosmer, Stephen T. (2001). *The Conflict Over Kosovo: Why Milosevic Decided to Settle When He Did*, Santa Monica: RAND Corporation

Hysa, Ylber (2004). "Kosovo: A Permanent International Protectorate?" in Edward Newman and Roland Rich (Eds.) *The UN Role in Promoting Democracy: Between Ideals and Reality*, New York: United Nations University Press

International Crisis Group (2007). *Kosovo – No Good Alternatives to the Ahtisaari Plan*, Europe Report No. 182, Brussels: ICG

International Civilian Office / *EU Special Representative. Mission Statement*. Available from http://www.ico-kos.org/

Judah, Tim (2008). *Kosovo: What Everyone Needs to Know*, Oxford: Oxford University Press

KDI – Kosovo Democratic Institute (2008). *Round table discussion on elections system in Kosovo*. Available from: http://www.kdi-kosova.org/alb/index.php?subaction=showfull&id=1211992913&archive=1217642101&start_from=&ucat=&

Koha Ditore (2010). "Brukseli me Strategji te vet per Veriun e Kosoves" [Brussels has its own strategy for the North of Kosovo], 24 March 2010. Available from: http://www.kohaditore.com/index.php?cid=1,22,15649

KFOR (Kosovo Force). Available from http://www.nato.int/kfor/

Latawski, Paul, and Martin A. Smith, (2003). *The Kosovo crisis and the evolution of post-Cold War European Security*, Manchester: Manchester University Press

McKinnon, Catriona (2008). "Case Study: NATO's Intervention in Kosovo" in Catriona McKinnon (Ed.) *Issues in Political Theory*, Oxford: Oxford University Press

Muguruza, Cristina C. (2003). "The European Union and Humanitarian Intervention in Kosovo: A Test for the Common Foreign Policy" in Bieber, Florian and Zidas Daskalovski (Eds.) *Understanding the War in Kosovo*, London: Frank Cass Publishers

Narten, Jens (2008). "Dilemmas of Promoting Local Ownership: The Case of Postwar Kosovo," in Roland Paris and Timothy Sisk (Eds.) *The Dilemmas of Statebuilding: Confronting the contradictions of postwar peace operations*, London: Routledge

Paris, Roland (2002). "International Peacebuilding and the 'Mission Civilisatrice,'" *Review of International Studies*, Vol. 28 (4), pp.637-656

Perritt, Henry H. (2008). *Kosovo Liberation Army: The Inside Story of an Insurgency*, Chicago: University of Illinois Press

Pond, Elizabeth (2008). "The EU Test in Kosovo," *The Washington Quarterly*, 31 (4), pp. 97-112

Reveron, Derek S. (2002). "Coalition Warfare: The Commander's Role" *Defense & Security Analysis*, 18 (2), pp. 107–121

Samuels, K. and von Esiedel, S. (2004). "The Future of UN State-building: Strategic and Operational Challenges and the Legacy of Iraq", *International Peace Academy*. Available from: http://www.ipacademy.org/pdfs/FUTURE_OF_UN_STATE_BUILDING.pdf

Sullivan, Stacy (2007). *Be Not Afraid, for You Have Sons in America: How a Brooklyn Roofer Helped Lure the U.S. into the Kosovo War*, New York: St. Martin's Press

Tansey, O (2007) "Democratization without a State: Democratic Regime-building in Kosovo", *Democratization*, 14: 1, pp. 129 — 150

Telegrafi News Agency (2010). "Policia e EULEX-it bastis zyrat e MTPT-se" [EULEX Police raids offices of the Ministry of Transport and Telecommunications]. 28 April 2010. Available from: http://www.telegrafi.com/?id=2&a=8349

UN News Centre (2008). "Ban Ki-moon urges restraint by all sides after Kosovo declares independence" [19 February 2008]. Available from http://www.un.org/apps/news/story.asp?NewsID=25659&Cr=Kosovo&Cr1

UNDP (2009). Early Warning Report No. 24, Fast Facts (April 2009). Available from http://www.ks.undp.org/repository/docs/FF_24_English.pdf

UNDP (2009). Early Warning Report No. 26, Fast Facts (November 2009). Available from: http://www.ks.undp.org/repository/docs/Fast_Facts_26_English.pdf

UNOSEK (2007). UN Office of Special Envoy for Kosovo: Status Settlement Proposal. Available from http://www.unosek.org/unosek/en/statusproposal.html

UNMIK (2008). Fact Sheet. Available from http://www.unmikonline.org/docs/2008/Fact_Sheet_July_2008.pdf

Van Roermund, B. (2002). "Seizing Sovereignty: The Law of its Image" *Social Legal Studies*,11; pp. 395

World Bank (2009). Kosovo Joins World Bank Group Institutions, Press Release [29 June 2009] Available from http://web.worldbank.org/WBSITE/EXTERNAL/COUNTRI ES/ECAEXT/0,,contentMDK:22230081~menuPK:258604~pa gePK:2865106~piPK:2865128~theSitePK:258599,00.html

CHAPTER 2

Transforming Balkanized Cultures: Seeing Schools as Advocates for Change

Gordon MacKinnon

An Introduction: What it Means to Teach

It is easy for educators to lose sight of what it means to teach. There are countless daily responsibilities attached to life as a teacher. The record keeping, message sending, classroom upkeep, and curriculum work all weigh heavily, and often obscure the importance of schools and schooling, again not to students but to teachers. It is easy to get bogged down and forget the reasoning behind your choice of education as a profession. Most teachers, I would hope, enter Bachelor of Education programs with intentions of a career of self-sacrifice and community service. Teaching hadn't always appealed to me; however in 2005, after a year of teaching kindergarten in South Korea, I decided to be an educator. It was frustrating work, to be sure, yet there were impressions of dignity and social responsibility that surrounded teaching and resonated within me. Upon completion of my Education degree in Ottawa, I taught again in South Korea, two years in Colombia, and I have recently completed my Master of Education in Curriculum Studies and am teaching in Halifax, Nova Scotia.

Now more than ever I feel a call to action: throughout my travels, and in Canada, as well, I have witnessed injustice, conflict instead of peace building, and poor policy and decision-making. In many cultures education is heralded as the solution to these social ills. Unfortunately, it is usually all talk. Education is often neglected and demoted both financially and culturally. We have lost this awareness of priority concerning education, and after years of this demotion there needs to be reclamation, a paradigm shift. Healthy vibrant schools breed healthy vibrant communities. If students are embedded in practices of critical thinking and global citizenship, after several generations, peace can finally be something tangible, not an idyllic naiveté. To me, this is what it means to teach: to help guide students to a better understanding of human relationships and responsibility in order to build a better more sustainable, peaceful world.

I had the incredible opportunity to study for three weeks in Kosovo this past May and June, through a course entitled the Balkans Peace Program. Created by economics professor Faton Bislimi, a Kosovar currently teaching in Halifax at Mount Saint Vincent University, the program aims to provide opportunities for students to engage in discussion of conflict and peace, all within the borders of this young nation struggling to build, re-establish peace, and retain a global voice. Kosovo is a nation about which I had known very little in regards to its cultural and historical significance. In 1998, at seventeen years of age, I remember hearing about Kosovo in the nightly news, as footage of ruined towns and displaced peoples began to dominate television screens worldwide. Into the new millennium, little to no coverage of the area has been reaching mainstream North

American media. Kosovo has become yet another forgotten "trouble area" in the world to many Canadians and Americans. This year, at age thirty, the Balkans Peace Program fell into my lap, and it sounded perfect: three weeks studying peace building, but within the contexts of Kosovo, a post-conflict nation! I knew my concepts of peace and reconciliation would be challenged, and evolve more organically than in the Canadian Maritimes, a region that has experienced relatively little recent conflict. Nova Scotia has experienced its share of tension, don't get me wrong. Halifax, for instance, still suffers from the consequences of the forced relocation of black citizens in the 1960s from a neighbourhood called Africville. Yet seeing other areas of the world has shown me that my little Canadian province runs rather harmoniously. Through living in both South Korea and Colombia, two areas of the world very different from my upbringing, and two nations who have had their share of recent conflict and radical societal change, I have been nurturing a desire to broaden my perspectives and knowledge of the globe through firsthand experience. Hence I jumped at the chance to learn about Kosovo from Kosovars, and apply what I would learn to my life as both an educator and global citizen.

The idea of global citizenship, as seen through the work of Global Education theorists such as Pike, Selby, Kniep, and Hanvey, is relatively uncommon in Canadian schools. The idea is for people to stop compartmentalizing themselves into rigid identities based on border, ethnicity, or historical framework. Humanity should be more fluid than this, and global citizenship calls for an awareness of interconnectedness and sustainability. In order for concepts of global education (such as the stridence toward global citizenship) to be introduced and work effectively, schools must break away from mechanistic mind frames and shift to a more holistic paradigm. Under global education, lines between distinct and isolated subject areas blur. Teacher-centered classrooms become student-centered. Information is dissected instead of immediately accepted or memorized. Restorative justice and reconciliation are favoured over punishment and segregation. Teachers collaborate together across all grade levels and subject areas, instead of dividing themselves into sub-groups. Finally, critical thinking, a skill at the heart of any student-centered classroom, can be worked upon much easier when students are encouraged to seek connections, problems, and solutions. Certainly peace education can flourish in educational cultures that have embraced these positions.

Part of the reason why Global Education and the concept of "global citizenship" are not currently embedded in schools is that powerful sub-cultures divide members of school communities and betray the fundamentals supporting holistic education. Frankly, the organization of many schools constructs learning environments that quickly become stuck in cozy routines and low-levels of risk-taking. This is particularly evident in how teachers interact with one another; in the early 1990s, Canadian educators Andy Hargreaves and Robert Macmillan explored the notion of these "cultures of teaching". They refer to two extremes in which teachers can find themselves: isolation/individualism which has teachers working alone, with little sharing of ideas and resources. Picture a teacher eating alone in his classroom during every lunch period, with the door shut, as a means of escapism or out of resentment. This teacher probably receives little support from colleagues and administration, or has simply unattached himself from others by constraint or choice. Through whatever reason this occurs, the educational climate suffers from the isolation of teachers due to the stagnancy of ideas. Peace, for example, is a topic so broad and complicated that a teacher cannot approach it unaided, in solitude. Isolated teaching cultures cannot effectively dissect far-reaching global issues, such as peace. A teaching culture of collaboration can; it is one of support and progression, with teachers routinely helping one another, especially in terms of professional development. Peace education is difficult and intimidating, and needs the support of the entire school staff. Hargreaves and Macmillan believe a culture of collaboration is more positive than isolation, however unfortunately less common. Realistically, teaching cultures are not simply one or the other, yet many schools produce teaching cultures that lean more toward isolation than collaboration. Cooperation and solidarity amongst teachers are essential for Global Education to work in schools, and for peace to be a topic that can be studied effectively.

Interestingly, Hargreaves and Macmillan explore the term 'Balkanization', describing it as a more specific teaching culture than isolation or collaboration. Like the Balkans, which saw the former Yugoslavia fragment into ethnically based nations (including Kosovo) in the 1990s with the fall of Communism, Balkanization of schools sees teachers and students working together but in specific sub-groups. Science teachers primarily collaborating with other science teachers is an example of how many teachers fragment into cultures based on a variety of reasons, age, subject area, experience, grade level, to name a few.

This segmentation, or Balkanization, is primarily seen as negative, and has been applied to many facets of global societies, not just education. Balkanization induces feelings of miscommunication and rigidity, of prejudice and xenophobia. It certainly is unfortunate for those living in the Balkans, that this area of the world evokes such negative connotations! Although I must admit, having lived in Kosovo, albeit for only three weeks, this fragmentation is almost immediately obvious; driving through a small town, if you see a mosque it is likely an area dominated by Muslim Albanians. If the town has a church, it probably has a predominant Orthodox Serbian population. Most noticeably to me, schools are also ethnically segregated in

Kosovo. For instance, I studied at Gjilani University College, a privately funded institution in the small city of Gjilan, outside the capital of Prishtina. The university has no Serbian students. The Albanian students who attend the university, and the program lectures in the Balkan Peace Program, admitted to me of only "knowing" Serbians. A Serb fixed my bike, once, for example. Ties between Serbs and Albanians seem to mostly end there, with little chance of deeper more meaningful connections being formed.

Sadly, and I suppose it is not surprising, I have been able to locate many connections between the Hargreaves and Macmillan article on Balkanization and my own experience in Kosovo (and Albania, Macedonia, and Montenegro, which I visited briefly). While the central focus of the article is on school culture, much of how they describe Balkanized-teaching cultures could easily depict the Balkan region of 2012. Fragmentation and hardened identities remain. The article was written in 1992, however, the year when conflict began in Bosnia and Herzegovina between Orthodox Bosnian Serbs (and Catholic Croats) and Muslim Bosniaks. In 1995, while entering adolescence, I recall watching footage of the Massacre of Srebrenica on CBC's The National, in horror. Grisly images of mass graves and evidence of "ethnic cleansing", a term I had never heard until that time, were merciless. I remember failing to grasp how people could do such things to one another. Some fifteen years later, after seeing the area with my own eyes, and the resulting repercussions from decades of conflict and tension, I am still at a loss.

My time in the Balkans was one of the most emotionally chaotic of my life. Every gracious gesture from the Albanian family that took me in was matched with some implausible tale from the war. I marvelled at the natural beauty of the country, and then rubbed my eyes in weary confusion over the complications of post-conflict development. When asked by people at home what I was learning, I began to ramble and rant, talking in circles and probably making little sense. I was so frustrated with humanity, and our inability to deny history its knack for repeating itself. I felt very low. After three weeks in the Balkans, however, when the course had finished, I spent some time in Berlin. I had never been before, and I was determined to see it after several recommendations from friends who believed I would fall in love with it. I certainly did, however for reasons which surprised me. Considering what I had just experienced, I was very conscious of how this city, once segregated by a giant wall, has dealt with a very violent recent history. The clouds parted within minutes of my first glimpse of the Memorial to the Murdered Jews of Europe; it encompasses an entire square block of central Berlin. It's also near Brandenburg Gate, the site in which East and West Berlin first united again, after decades of separation, with the first hammer blows to destroy the Berlin Wall. The area must have been (and still is) prime real estate. Yet instead of constructing skyscrapers, the city of Berlin built a large memorial to remember the victims of Adolf Hitler and Nazism. You can enter the memorial from all sides. There are no gates or fences or ticket booths; it is easily accessible, day or night. There are signs explaining why it was built the way it was. I was moved by the fact that it is not only wheelchair accessible, but made so in sobering reference to the thousands of physically disabled people who were murdered during the war. To me, by building this memorial in the center of the city, Berlin is committed to open and honest discourse in regards to its past. The memorial serves as a constant reminder to Berliners that the Holocaust happened, and that everyone is responsible to ensure that it never happens again.

Upon my arrival home in Halifax, Mount Saint Vincent professor Sherida Hassanali asked me to speak at a summer peace education conference in Pugwash, Nova Scotia. I, of course, eagerly agreed as I saw this as a chance for me to collect my rather scattered contemplations on my time in Kosovo. While Berlin focused my energy and sense of social responsibility in terms of peace, I was still puzzled as to how my experience in Kosovo would impact my teaching, and overall trajectory as an educator. A peace education conference was just the ticket! Pugwash is home to the Thinker's Lodge, a beautiful Victorian house perfectly positioned on the quiet shores of the

Northumberland Strait. It was the summer home of highly successful Canadian businessman Cyrus Eaton, a man who later developed into an astute philanthropist. He became intensely aware of the relationship between education and social improvement, and wanted his summer home to be a center to strengthen this connection. As a native to the area, I can attest to the sense of ease that breathes into the soul of any creature lucky enough to spend time on the northern coast of Nova Scotia, and I am certainly not surprised that Eaton saw his home in Pugwash as an ideal location to have people come, relax, and then meet and discuss important issues surrounding peace. I was in dire need of this.

My Time in Kosovo: Retrospect and Revelations

In preparation for my presentation, in which I had a mere 2 weeks to arrange, I had time to finally digest my time in Kosovo. I arrived on a Sunday in Prishtina, and was greeted by the youngest son of my host family, Alban. The tall, lanky 21-year old immediately began to ask questions about Canada and my life there, as well as explain various aspects of the city that he assumed I was observing and attempting to make sense of. He was very confident, not only in his English, but in his manner of expressing opinion. I knew we would be great friends. As I mentioned before, I knew little about Kosovo prior to my arrival.

I had read that for European standards, the new nation is both very young and very poor. This is almost immediately apparent, from the first steps into the Adem Jashari International Airport; the atmosphere was young, feisty, and gritty. Flights to and from major cities in Germany, Austria, and Switzerland, instead of cities in neighbouring countries like Albania and Macedonia, reveal a staggering fact: most Kosovars live outside of Kosovo, mainly in these Western European nations, working and wiring money home to family. Most Kosovars I spoke with had members of their family living abroad, including my host brother Alban; at the time of my sojourn, his father was working as a mechanic in Afghanistan. His family lives in relative comfort, however I could tell the father was sorely missed.

In true Albanian form, I was treated like royalty in the home of my host family. Guests and wanderers can expect to be fed and sheltered without much hesitation by Kosovar households. Off a busy one-lane residential street, Alban led me down a driveway, past a few old cars and a pretty garden of flowers and vegetables, to his home. His grandparents live in the bottom part of the house, and he and his mother, father, and older brother live above. His brother speaks a little English, however his mother, none. Alban learned to speak English from his father, who from what I have been told has a fine command of the language. I had practiced a few pleasantries in Albanian to last me through the first few days of introductions. They didn't really help me aside from showing everyone that I was attempting to communicate in their mother tongue. It is rather uncomfortable to be led into a stranger's house in which you will stay for a significant amount of time. I was given a bedroom with a massive bed, decorated with various charms and knickknacks. I had never seen a room like it, and I initially felt like somewhat of an intruder. I was abruptly stopped if I tried to clear the dinner table, and I became overly conscious of using up items such as hot water and toilet paper.

Over time, and after quite a few awkward family dinners and jumbled exchanges, I began to feel at home and truly enjoy my time with my host family; reading in the garden, greeting Alban's affectionate grandparents every morning, eating Albanian meats, pastries, and other Albanian cuisine items served up fresh by Alban's gracious and generous mother. I would go out often with Alban to chat over very strong macchiato. Like most Albanian Kosovars, he does not consume alcohol, so we drank coffee. Cafes are common and smoky and attended primarily by 20 and 30 something males. He and I would talk mainly about Kosovo, and he revealed his frustrations with how his country has been run in the past thirteen years, post-conflict. This time has been tough on Kosovo, especially in terms of its economic recovery. The nation imports far more than it exports, leaving a population entrenched in high unemployment, forcing many, again, to leave the country for greener and more lucrative pastures. On one evening, I entered the home of one family with five adult children, all of who were living at home and without jobs. While they were as pleasant and accommodating as any other family I encountered, the strain was evident and heartbreaking. I left their home with the exchanges of frustration I had had with Alban ruminating within me, raw and unmovable.

Alban and I biked to his (private, Albanian) university nearly every morning. We borrowed the bicycles from his uncle and cousin, who use them every day but insisted we take them for the duration of my stay in Kosovo. The ride to school was beautiful: rolling mountains and dusty trails, through the untouched green spaces of the city, led us to the private university. The university consists of only one building, and apparently like many private universities in Kosovo, has a reputation of being too easy. While I did not feel at any point like I was in a climate of astute academia, students seemed proud to be attending university and shared their aspirations with me often. Classes were held for three weeks, with each class being about 3 or 4 hours long. I was one of five international students, with the majority of the class comprised of students from the university who wanted to experience a class in English, with English-speakers. We mainly talked about peace development and peace building, with the relationship of Kosovo and its neighbours at the center of these discussions. Most of the

Kosovar students were between the ages of 18 and 21. They were very young when the war of 1998/1999 occurred, and with the exception of Alban, most spoke very little of the conflict and how it was for them as young children. With this generation in particular, there does seem to be a detachment from this recent violent history. Understandably, they are concerned first and foremost with employment, whether it is in Kosovo or abroad. With Kosovo struggling to create new jobs, it seems like the former option is too often the case.

With many students shy to express themselves in English, most of the discussions involved us, the international students, eager to make sense of our host country and its economic, social, and historical decisions. I left every class understanding a bit more, and each left me thinking all day long. Yet there was one class in particular that I will never forget, for the sole reason that it left me completely bewildered. We were talking about education in Kosovo, which of course had me in high alert. Previous to the class, I had visited a school near to where I was living with Alban. It was in the shape of a 'T', apparently after Tito, the leader of Yugoslavia throughout most of its existence. I sat in on an English class, and was charmed by the students and teachers. The school obviously lacked resources and a steady curriculum, however it was there, running, and full of life. I met with the principal, who seemed very proud of his school and the fact that I was there and interested. All was going well until he exclaimed that it was a shame that Canada has allowed so many people from different cultures to immigrate and be burdensome to the educational system. With Alban translating (the principal did not speak English), I may have mistaken his meaning, however it became apparent to me that schools in Kosovo are homogenous, ethnically and linguistically speaking, for reasons that I cannot understand.

So I entered this discussion on education in Kosovo with already a lot of questions. Our professor revealed that it has been mandated that all schools in Kosovo must teach English. This makes sense, it is the language that has been forced on many to learn for quite some time, and in 2012, you are better off knowing it than not. However, I wondered if there was any attempt for schools, segregated by ethnicity, to allow Albanian students to learn the Serbian language, and vice versa. It made perfect sense in my head: in order to overcome a conflict, you must be able to communicate to 'the other'. Not only are Albanians and Serbs separated physically, in the layout of neighborhoods and schools, but they are isolated by language, as well. It seemed ridiculous to me that if they were to talk to one another, they would have to do so in English. The thought of Albanians and Serbs speaking to each other in their native tongues in appreciation of this effort to learn from one another warmed my heart. So I raised my hand and asked if there is any movement within schools in Kosovo, to not only learn English, but languages that regionally would allow for more cultural boundaries to be crossed. I received a flat "No", in which I responded with a condensed explanation of my above thinking. An Albanian student, a man in his late 20s, raised his hand to respond. He had fought in the war as a young man of 17. He expressed that he could not learn the Serbian language, that speaking it reminded him of what he lived through in the 1990s. He told us that he held his best friend in his arms, dying from a Serb bullet. I felt awful. Here I was, a relatively privileged Canadian having no idea what it was to live through violence of this extreme, expressing ideas through my lens of Celebrating Multiculturalism and Diversity, to people who have endured centuries of ethnic division and conflict. I do not know what it is like to have my best friend die in my arms.

I left the class grappling with this: the idea of learning a neighbour's language seems level-headed, theoretically speaking. Yet, how can it work when there is so much history and so many hard feelings? There is so much unresolved grief in Kosovo. Outside the Parliament buildings in Prishtina, there is a fence with photos of some of the 2,000+ people still missing from the war. People have attached these faces in despairing attempt to find out anything about missing loved ones. Walking by the fence makes one conscious of the fragility of human life and relationships. I breathed heavily as I passed, making eye contact with many of the faces of the disappeared. Life slows down considerably when you contemplate grief of this magnitude.

In the next class we tackled some important questions: How does one move on, and most importantly, how can one forgive? If either of these questions is left unanswered, I feel like this region is doomed to fall back into conflict. We decided to deconstruct a diagram by David Steele, entitled "Cycles of Victimhood and Transformation: Destructive versus Constructive." Its purpose is to demonstrate the paths people take in dealing with grief. It uses two circles, one enveloping the other. They are attached at one point, the realization of loss. From this point, some people follow the inside circle, suppressing grief and creating myths. This leads to a desire for revenge, and ultimately, a return to conflict. Or, a person can express grief, confront fears, and travel a road to reconciliation. We all agreed that the diagram is too simple, as one must anticipate a great deal of complexity when dealing with grief, i.e. people may maneuver back and forth, in both circles, on his or her way to either reconciliation or conflict. However, the diagram does reveal a certain degree of truth in how grieving persons handle themselves in these deeply affecting times. One student offered that perhaps the choice of path is gendered. It is no big secret that in many cultures males are conditioned to suppress emotion, that to be emotionally vulnerable is weak or effeminate. Considering that males dominate most government and military positions, it could be argued that many people making decisions in regards to war and peace have not grieved in a way that re-humanizes 'the other'.

Another factor that this model does not take into account at all is the complexity of the grief experienced. It may be easier for me, one who has experienced little in the way of violent conflict, to follow the road to reconciliation with another who has caused me grief. Many Canadians, including myself, do not have centuries of conflicted history that are still relevant in their day to day lives; if a loved one is killed by a person with whom you have little to no historical connection with, it makes sense that the healing process will be a little less complicated. You do not have to contend with pre-existing attitudes and stereotypes that would otherwise cloud an already difficult situation. The Albanian student who could not bring himself to speak Serbian has been left to grieve for his friend within the messy milieu of current Albanian-Serb relations. Like many conflicts caused by ethnic division, history and myth intermingle in the aftermath, which in turn can be manipulated by powerful systems like media and government. Both sides of the conflict have a "right side of history." I did not have many chances to interact with many Serbs, and I wish I had. While I did not hear any Albanian Kosovars speak hatefully about Serbia, I only heard their accounts of the war. While I do not for a second question the atrocities performed by Serbs on Albanians as being untrue or any less devastating, I do wish I had been able to hear from Serbs about how they lived through the war. There must be overlap, in sorrow and loss. There must be common ground. However in Kosovo, Albanians and Serbs have grieved in isolation from one another: a Serb cemetery here, an Albanian monument there. Overall you get the feeling that the country hasn't come together to move forward. There seems to be very little reconciliation between the two ethnic groups.

Take for instance, the home of Adem Jashari; first of all, this man's image can be seen everywhere in Kosovo, and it's not just any old portrait. Always in full army camouflage, touting rifles and other artillery, the bearded leader of the Kosovo Liberation Army (KLA) is a prominent face in Kosovo. The international airport is named after him, equipped with the same large hyper-militaristic image of this now national (Albanian) hero. One afternoon we traveled to his former house. In 1998, he and most of his family partook in a grisly 3-day battle with the Serb army. Staked out within the confines of the house, each family member save one (daughter Besarta) met their fate by a Serb bullet or shell. Adem Jashari was also killed. The house has not been restored, so one immediately is startled by its condition: bullet holes, graffiti, burned out inside. It has become something of a tourist attraction, with the graves of the members of the Jashari family ordered in a beautiful monument across the road from the house. I noticed that one of them was born in 1981, the year of my birth. I began recalling what I was doing in March of 1998, at 17 years of age. There were many children running around the house, laughing and carrying on. This left me utterly confused, having just heard the history of what had gone down in this house a mere thirteen years prior, that anyone could be having fun in the vicinity. I listened in horror as our guide described how Besarta was forced to identify the bodies of her fallen family members. The children continued to play as I attempted to contemplate this horrific series of events. Even the adults present seemed to be enjoying themselves. I found a place to sit down to digest all of this, and flipped through the tourist guide, which had been translated into English. It was sensational, to be sure; poorly translated, and using a lot of accusatory language towards Serbs. It really hit me in that moment that I did not understand this war. I did not understand war in general.

A   At times, living in Kosovo, peace seemed a hopeless case to me. On this day in particular, I left the Adem Jashari house in emotional and mental disarray, struggling to make sense of the human race. I had felt similar when the Albanian student in class expressed his feelings about speaking Serbian. I understand where this student was coming from. A Serb had killed his best friend. However, I am sure there are Serbs who would share similar stories if I had had the chance to communicate with them. Yet Serbs are internationally known as the aggressors in this case. Slobodan Milosevic and other Serb leaders are responsible for the planning and execution, literally, of many ethnic groups in the Balkan region. I get it, and I wish he had been brought to justice instead of dying from a heart attack before the verdict. Albanians continue to feel like second-class citizens in 2012, with Serb Kosovars exempt from paying electricity and following car license regulations, no doubt in an attempt by the government and the EU to simply keep the peace.

There is so much injustice. Yet, this is not what I grapple with the most. I fundamentally cannot understand why people with differences cannot coexist in respect and cooperation. Why do we separate and isolate out of difference? Why do we succumb to "Balkanization"? Why is any other way considered naïve or "not how the world works"? We've walked on moon, why can't we end conflict? While living in Kosovo, this line of questioning evoked strong feelings within me. At times, for the sake of my own sanity, I had to escape into a novel or film. This may explain why so many Kosovars were enjoying themselves at the Jashari house: in front of us was a heap of bullet-ridden concrete, screaming its violent history. Digging deep into our emotional pasts is difficult work. For many Kosovars, perhaps all they want to be is happy again, to concentrate on the future after so many years of suffering. It makes sense, and my heart aches for them. For me, however, an outsider, I yearn to witness signs of truth and reconciliation.

We arrived in the village of Krusha e Madhe shortly after our visit to the house of Adem Jashari. We were in three cars, so navigation was tricky, and even more so when we arrived in the area and could not find the exact village. We stopped and asked for directions several times, but it took someone jumping in the car to direct for us to finally reach Krusha. In 1998, in what took just twenty four hours, the Serb army shot and killed most of the teenage and adult Albanian males living in the village. The bodies were burned in the woods. It was warm and sunny when we arrived, yet I could not shake the chill that continued to flow through my body when in Krusha. With such unimaginable tragedy falling upon one village, Krusha is actually more well-known for something entirely more positive: it is home to one of Kosovo's only successful export, a preservative spread made from red peppers that are farmed in the region. After the war, the women of the community began an agricultural co-op, eventually leading to this business. I began to see the spread in grocery stores and markets throughout Kosovo. I still cannot determine which is more baffling: for a community to have to endure that much grief, or for these women to be that resilient. The short hour we spent with the women, who proudly showed us their small workshops and bottling rooms, counts as one of the most inspirational moments of my life. This is what it means to take control of one's fate, to not allow conflict and hatred to determine how your life unfolds. While I could tell these women still suffer from a great deal of sadness, they have channeled their suffering into something that I daresay was beautiful to behold. Despite their horrific shared history, these women are a Kosovo success story.

How Education Can Transform

The peace education conference at Thinker's Lodge allowed me to deconstruct my experience in Kosovo. I have changed, without question, as a person and as an educator. Yet it brought something out inside me, which I felt intensely when I first began to explore what it meant to teach, but had dimmed over the years. Education can inspire change. I know Kosovars want to change their country. They want to be free from conflict. They want to be known internationally for something besides a recent war. I know this because this is what has been expressed to me by Kosovars. However, in order for this to happen, schools and school systems need to be stronger. Education should be a priority in post-conflict countries. Students should learn about peace, and how to be peaceful. Students should learn how to communicate effectively to one another, and how to listen. We had the opportunity to speak with a few people of notable status in the political spectrum in Kosovo, and when asked by myself about the education system, one replied that it was a mess and needed assistance. While I am not in a position at the moment to be giving governments advice on how to structure their education system, there are a few points that have come to me in regards to peace education since my stay in Kosovo.

First, students must learn to how to grapple with change. Many classrooms are built so that students will always arrive to the correct answer eventually, whether it is independently or through the help of another. Many problems do not have an easy solution. They are messy. Students must learn to anticipate complexity when grappling with global issues, and also learn to be comfortable with leaving a class without an answer. To some, this experience induces anxiety and frustration. The process of solving problems is often uncomfortable, yet students must take risks in order to move forward. In general, schools do not provide enough opportunities for students to grapple and brood and struggle. It is in these times when they can reach enlightenment, as I did in my time away and in the weeks following at home in Canada. I left many classes in Kosovo puzzled and anxious, yet through communication, internally and with others, I have come to see that Kosovo is the same as any other place on this Earth; that a nation is only as strong as its education system. Young people must learn how to be global citizens. They must learn how to deal with change. And in essence, they must learn how to learn.

They must also learn how to grieve. Kosovars have not had enough opportunities for their voices to be heard. Like the

Truth and Reconciliation process that is currently happening in Canada amongst its aboriginal peoples and communities, people who have suffered must have a voice. Expressing grief openly and honestly is a crucial part of the healing process. Alban, my host brother, is good at this; he is often frustrated, to be sure, about the state of his country and the dips and turns it takes on the way to becoming a peaceful independent nation. He misses his father who works abroad. He wants Kosovo to be more autonomous. He wishes Albanians and Serbs would get along. He thinks back on his life as a young boy in a war-torn land with great deal of sadness. But he has allowed himself to be open to new ideas, and he is always willing to express his emotions without shame or self-pity. It is never direct, always fluctuating, but it is a healthy grieving process. If this does not happen, creation of stereotypes and prejudice continues, and both sides argue its "right side of history". If you search for information on the 1998-1999 conflict in Kosovo on the Internet you will find varying accounts of what happened. Unsurprisingly, Albanian and Serb authors differ tremendously in their opinions. To my knowledge, there hasn't been much of a coming together between the two groups to reach a common ground. None at all, I would imagine. Yet I think it is clear that if peace is to ever sustain in the region, this must happen. If this is not going to happen at the government level, then it must happen at local levels, and where else for that to occur but in schools. Students should have opportunities to explore emotion, strong emotions like grief, hatred, and forgiveness. They should develop their emotional intelligence. Finally, they should learn how to communicate effectively with 'the other', in the direction of re-humanization.

Finally, schools must emphasize the importance of learning from the past. Berlin decided to build a giant memorial in the middle of the city as a constant reminder of their past. It is a pledge that the Holocaust will never happen again in Germany. Seeing this reminded me, that as an educator I am able to promote critical deconstruction of the past. In a recent Grade 7 science class we talked about Lake Victoria in Africa, and how the introduction of a large predacious fish 60 years prior had seemed like a good idea at the time (by the non-Africans who did this), but soon led to the extinction of many of the native species of fish in the lake. We decided that the decision was made too hastily, and that solutions to this problem must be thought out with care. My students were grappling with this issue, weighing the disastrous environmental consequences with the clear economic gain that has turned Lake Victoria into Africa's most important inland fishing locale. Students need to see past decisions and why they were made. They must see that many solutions are complicated. Yet, as long as we look to the past to inform the present (and predict the future), then repeating mistakes becomes less likely.

In my class in Kosovo, I learned that half of the world's post-conflict countries fall back into conflict after five years. There is still unrest in the northern region of Mitrovica, as it borders Serbia and is still hotly contested. The rest of Kosovo is relatively safe and stable. Yet I worry about that region, and the friends that I made in such a quick amount of time. I believe in the leadership of Kosovars, that they will strengthen schools and provide young generations with plenty of chances to study the past, and learn from it. I realize that the stability of the region depends greatly on relations with Serbia, and at the moment, there are virtually none. Serbia still claims Kosovo as within their borders, and denounces its declaration of independence in 2008. Presently there are over 90 countries that recognize Kosovo's autonomy. This makes travel very complicated for Kosovars, and many of my friends and classmates, understandably, expressed frustration to me about this. I do not know Serbia's intentions, nor can I comprehend its reasoning for continuing to be aggressive towards Albanians. I did not spend any time in Serbia. I did not speak with any Serbs in Kosovo in any depth; about their lives or how they perceive the actions the government of Serbia are taking in the name of their people. For my experience in the Balkans to be, and I hesitate to use this word, complete, I think this needs to happen.

I do know that Balkanization is a truly unfortunate word. It is using a collection of states, peoples and communities to describe a variety of negative and degenerating policies and frameworks. These people have suffered enough as it is to be handled in this manner by the academic world. So let us cease using this term, and instead focus on the following ways of asserting ourselves positively: critical thinking, reconciliation, and building commitment to not repeat mistakes. And in my eyes, education must be held high and challenged. If the Balkans is to ever shake off its image as the "powder keg of Europe", then above all trust, between neighbours, towns, and states, must be fostered whenever possible - a re-humanization of "the other". I met some truly remarkable individuals while in Kosovo, who have changed my life for the better. I am happier. I am more focused. I am more thankful. And I will certainly not allow myself to lose sight of what it means to be an educator. My good friend Alban expressed to me once that he wants for Kosovars, of all ethnicities, to stand up together and say, "this is my country, and I want to live here." I cheer his vision and echo his sentiments. We don't have to fight, and we don't have to hate. We are capable of so much more.

References:

Hanvey, R. (1982). An attainable global perspective. *Theory into Practice*, 21(3), 162-167.

Hargreaves, A., Macmillan, R. (1992). *Balkanized Secondary Schools and the Malaise of Modernity.* The Ontario Institute for Studies in Education

Kniep, W. M. (1989). Social studies within a global education. *Social Education,* 53(6), 399-403.

Krastev, I. (2002). 'The Balkans: Democracy without Choices.' *Journal of Democracy,* 13 (3), 39-50.

Steele, David. (2009). 'A Manual to Facilitate Conversations of Religious Peace Building and Reconciliation.' Retrieved from: http://www.humiliationstudies.org/whoweare/board03.php

CHAPTER 3

Kosovo—Where Optimism and Hope Never Die

Laura Lussier

WHEN sending in my application for the Balkans Peace Program, some of my concerns were that if I were to be accepted, it would both be my first trip to Europe, as well as my first time travelling alone. Both these thoughts were terrifying enough in themselves, but were amplified due to my limited knowledge of Kosovo and the surrounding areas that we were to visit. My knowledge consisted, at the time, of a few internet researches that turned up such images as war scenes, heavy international presence and poverty. However, these images were not enough to deter me from travelling across the Atlantic Ocean to a country that was war-stricken only 13 years ago. The truth is that I was hopeful, hopeful that I would witness something different than what was portrayed online. To say the least, I was not disappointed by the Republic of Kosovo and its people.

Even though it is not the case, many people still regard Kosovo as being a dangerous place even after 13 years of peace. An example of this fear would be the Russian man who sat beside me on my first flight. His exact words when told him I was travelling to Kosovo were "don't go there, it is a scary place." However, this man was from Russia, a main factor for the continued struggle of Kosovo regarding its recognition as an independent country. Russia, which is one of the five permanent members of the United Nations Security Council, continues to promise to veto all suggestions regarding Kosovo and its independent status. The issue of independence is a sensitive one for the ethnic Albanians who live in the country. Kosovo used to be part of the country of Serbia, which was originally part of communist Yugoslavia before it crumbled, and was inhabited both my Serbs and Albanians. However, there was heavy inequality within the region between both ethnicities, the Albanians had been getting the short end of the stick for decades. A lack of investment within the region also caused tensions with the Serbian capital, Belgrade. In the 1990s, tension mounted and eventually war broke out between the Albanian Kosovars and Serbia. From 1998 to 1999, there was war throughout Kosovo, killing thousands and leaving the Kosovars with many problems that are still present today. An example of this is the poverty that is apparent everywhere, from the litter strewn across the country to the little economic development that Kosovo has seen since 1999. There is also still tension between the Serbs who remained in Kosovo and the ethnic Albanians, who identify more with their neighbour Albania than with their own country.

During the war, NATO, led by the United States of America, intervened in Kosovo after Serbia refused to give in to diplomatic measures and in order to stop the fighting, bombed Serbia for 78 days in a row. An International Protectorate was declared on June 12th, 1999 and the United Nations took charge of administering the country. For almost 10 years, the people of Kosovo did not really belong to any country since Kosovo was governed by international institutions. However, as of February 17th 2008, the Republic of Kosovo declared its independence and is currently recognized by approximately 90 UN-member countries. However, since it is technically not a "real country" due to the refusal of recognition by the Security Council, Kosovars cannot participate in such things as the Olympics or even FIFA. Kosovo still only has a special envoy to the UN as its representation. Thus, Kosovo still seems to be in a sort of limbo. It is a country in itself, with a functioning government and institutions, yet it is not because it does not have the power or the rights of an internationally recognized state.

After the war, Kosovo became the poorest country in Europe and still has the lowest average salary. This was one thing that you could tell simply by walking in the streets. There is an overt amount of poverty visible in cities and in the countryside. At 2 o'clock in the afternoon on a weekday, there were people wandering everywhere, wasting time in cafés. The majority of the population of Kosovo is idle. With about 45% of Kosovars unemployed, this is not surprising. Even on construction sites, there would be a maximum of 5-6 workers attempting to build an entire structure. There seemed to be stagnation, even where there was development.

When I first arrived in the Republic of Kosovo, our hosts, Adelina and Elvira, immediately wished to introduce Jessica, a fellow participant from Halifax, and me to some of their friends. We also met Elvira's fiancé, Niti. We were rapidly immersed into what is called the "café culture", where you hop from little café to little café. Some days, participants and their hosts could go to five different locations, just to grab a coffee. By the end of a few days, we were almost dependent and pretty much wired constantly. Our café experience that first day was one of novelties for me: a small Turkish coffee, the Albanian language spoken quickly around me, as well as my first marriage proposal. Apparently, as a young, single foreigner I was quite a catch to some men. Marriage seemed to be one of those things that happen at a young age in Kosovo, a Muslim country where sex before marriage is frowned upon by many.

When I arrived at the house of my host family, the Jerlius, I was immediately greeted as a member their family, with a few special attentions that I was determined to get rid of. They first asked me if my parents had been made aware of my safe arrival in Kosovo. To my negative response, I received a reaction: "Wouldn't they worry? Don't you care? Hurry! Call them, email them!" It was quite a big deal. This was my first taste of the collective, family-oriented culture that is found in Kosovo, which was to be my home for the next three weeks. Being a person who enjoys being alone a large deal, as well as coming from an individualistic society made for a combination that was not very well understood by my hosts or by their neighbours— their cousins, aunts and uncles, and grand-parents.

I had actually gotten to choose my family and was more than pleased. I had two brothers to tease and who spoke English, Arlind and Blendi, as well as Adelina, and their parents. My host mother unfortunately did not speak English, but we managed to communicate through sign language and eventually, with a few Albanian words that I learned. Otherwise, we laughed it off and I would be dragged to the object of our attempted conversation. As for my host father, he wasn't around very much in my opinion, working in a building as some sort of engineer most of the day. He spoke English and had travelled to the United States before, which was much more than the vast majority of Kosovars could say they could and had done. Arlind, an 18 year-old high school graduate with big dreams and ideas, became a great source of information and companionship since he was interested very much in practicing his English and in correcting my ways. Blendi, my 15 year-old little brother, is the sweetest boy that I had the pleasure of meeting in Kosovo. Blendi helps out his mother around the house, encouraged me to play sports with him and his cousins, and just has the most genuine love for everybody. Finally, Adelina was my official host. At 21 years old, she is the typical girly-girl, which I am not, but was so welcoming and friendly that, in spite of our differences, we were close during my stay.

From the alley, my host family's house looked similar to many other buildings that I had observed in Gjilan, the town where we stayed. However, once inside, it was obvious that the Jerlius were wealthy: multiple televisions and laptops, a great bathroom and many other details contributed to this impression. Poverty, the problem of thousands of Kosovars, was not found in the Jerliu household or in any of the homes of the other hosts. The Balkans Peace Program was put in place by the Bislimi Group Foundation in cooperation with the Gjilani University College, a private institution, which explains the relative economic ease of the Kosovar participants.

During our first week, I met my fellow foreign participants: Jessica, Gordie, Andrew and Masayuki. Most of us were from Canada, all studying in Halifax with the exception of myself who hailed from the French-speaking province of Quebec. We spent much of our time discussing how we felt about our experience and created solid bonds between each other. Often, our hosts would take breaks from speaking English, which was difficult and limiting for the majority of them, and leave us to chat amongst ourselves. For me, meeting these special people was a revelation because it finally brought me closer to individuals who shared my interests and excitement vis-à-vis adventure, developing countries and moving out of our comfort zone. During our three weeks together, I truly felt like the person I wanted to be. Without anything holding me back, I honestly felt like myself in Kosovo.

The first half of the Balkans Peace Program consisted of a course on post-conflict peace building, using the specific example of Kosovo most of the time. Professor Faton Bislimi headed the class for a couple of hours every day and we learned about many of the problems found in the country. The background of the Kosovo War of 1998-1999 was explained to us. The things that happened during the war, such as the immense displacement of the population, the destruction, and the deaths were also described to us. The horrors that so many innocent people beheld, only 13 years prior, were baffling for me. As a white, middle class Canadian citizen, the realities of the Kosovars seemed so far from my own.

Seeing the reactions of the Albanian students while discussing the situation of Kosovo before and during the war made my whole experience so much more personal and emotional. Often, I felt like the offenses and crimes against the Albanian people were my own. One day in class, we were discussing the events of the war and an older student mentioned that during the war, when he was around 15 or 16 years old, he had his best friend die in his arms. It was one of those difficult things to hear. This man had become a friend and to hear that he had gone through such events in his life, while we were in safety thousands of miles away, made it hard to hold back the tears. Silence came over the room after his declaration; you can't say much when you hear such a thing. Another day, we watched a documentary on the return of refugees to Kosovo. Over 1.5 million people returned to Kosovo within one week of its liberation from Serbian forces, only to find death and destruction everywhere. During the video, the BBP participants watched, stunned. Most of the Albanians did not pay much attention to the documentary, maybe attempting to block out the memories. However, one of our Albanian friends cried for his people. This was one of the saddest moments of my trip.

As mentioned, most of the Albanian students approached the course in an offhand manner. My theory was that they were trying to forget their past and move forward. It was that they seemed to want to forget that disturbed me. Embracing the events, accepting that they had happened and remembering them in order to never have them repeated is what seems to me as a solution. Denial of a devastating war may be one of the root causes for future conflict.

Professor Bislimi's course also introduced us to economic concepts related to development, which were familiar to me due to my background in international development studies. However, the main goal of the Balkans Peace Program and of our peace-building course was to teach us to not make the same mistakes as previous leaders had done, as well as to realize that there are still steps to take in order to achieve peace in Kosovo. The aims of peace-building are to end violence, but more importantly to create conditions so that violence does not return to a region. Although the complete elimination of violence has not been achieved in the northern region of Kosovo, it was peaceful and very safe in all the other areas we visited. However, it is the second aim that was an issue in our class and within our group of foreigners. In Kosovo, the conditions to keep conflict at bay have not been fully executed yet.

There remain many examples of tension in the Republic of Kosovo between the ethnic Albanians and the Serbs. Firstly, neither group speaks the language of the other. An example was given to me that when discussing the purchase of a motorcycle from a Serb by an Albanian, since they could not communicate in their mother tongues, they spoke German to each other. Both languages are the official languages of the country, but rarely will you find a Kosovar who can speak both. Secondly, the locations of Serbian villages are known and often Albanians will avoid them. For example, on our way to the capital of Pristina, we crossed a particular Serbian village. Every single time we went by, the town was pointed out to us as if it were an anomaly in the landscape. The differences could be seen, but so could the differences in attitude. Finally, there is inequality in the treatment of the Serbs and the Albanians in order to appease the minority group of Serbs. This is mainly due to a treaty signed after the war. One of the main examples we were given was that the Serbs receive free electricity, while the Albanians do not. Many other instances exemplifying tensions occurred over the course of our trip however.

Our first week was full of introductions and new friends. Our hosts wished for us to meet most of their families and many of their friends, so we travelled through town quite a bit. On the first day, I was encouraged to attend my host brother, Arlind's, English class. It was a class with about twenty students in it, all paying for private English lessons at a small school. They were very interested to hear me speak, just to hear my accent and how easily the words came to me. These students were in the highest level and were truly excellent. They discussed important themes during their classes, could explain almost all the exceptions of the English language, as well as conjugate every verb near perfectly according to each situation. On technical terms, they had almost mastered the English language, especially compared to me. Meeting these students was a great experience for me. These students believed that speaking English was the solution to upward mobility, for themselves and for their country. They had the economic resources to improve their positions and found a solution to do so.

Another Albanian friend of mine, Albulena also known as Lena, spoke English almost perfectly as well, the best English I heard from a young Kosovar to be exact. She had learned simply from watching American movies. This was a method that many Albanian Kosovars use to learn new languages, such as English, Spanish and Turkish. It works because watching television also helped with my comprehension of the Albanian language. After much criticism directed at the Canadians for not trying to learn Albanian, Elvira's 10 year old brother, Ensar, taught me many basic words in the language. We communicated by pointing at objects or by making gestures and him telling me the word in Albanian, then I repeated in English for him. In this manner, my vocabulary increased immensely. However, it was not enough. Learning the Albanian alphabet and all the various sounds permitted me to gain fundamental reading skills. Then when watching the news on television with my host family, I would read aloud the titles and subtitles that would display along the screen. My comprehension and pronunciation were getting better and better, but Arlind and Blendi would still laugh their heads off at my efforts.

One thing that I did notice during my time in Kosovo was how entrenched in society gender roles seemed to be. Women stayed home, cooked and took care of their husbands. Men went to work, were the providers, had to be strong. Being a bit of a tomboy and very independent, I didn't fit in very well according to my host brother, Arlind. He often teased me about how I dressed like a boy, meaning wearing loose clothing and little makeup, and about the fact that I would want to play sports, which isn't normal for a girl my age. It was true that most girls, except a handful, were very feminine, wearing cute outfits all the time and lots of cosmetics. As opposed to in Canada, where I dress like the average girl, in Kosovo I was seen as being boyish. This also happened when I attempted to participate in soccer games and volleyball with Blendi and his cousins. My behaviour was abnormal for the Albanian Kosovars. Maybe I was simply walking too closely to the line defining gender. This most likely explains why the Albanian girls and I didn't have such a great connection; we were too different in some ways.

Meals in Kosovo marked me in our first week, as of my very first morning. Breakfast is completely different from a typical morning meal in Canada. To say the least, breakfast threw me off guard every single day and my hosts enjoyed my puzzled looks when I was served. This was because we would eat food that in my opinion should have been served either for lunch or dinner, such as tomatoes, cucumbers, and even chicken soup! Another day we had something which my hosts told me was chicken lungs. Honestly, every meal in Kosovo felt like an adventure. Food is eaten mostly with your fingers, which my good manners refused to accept most of the time. At every meal there is also bread, in various forms according to the whims of my host mother. As opposed to in Canada, where bread tends to compliment your meal, bread is a staple in Kosovar cooking. It was used both as a means of filling oneself and as basic part of every meal. Most occasions where I ate, I consumed traditional foods. Products that were typically found in each course were tomatoes, cucumbers, a sort of yogurt drink (that I found disgusting), bread, and a form of traditional white milky "sauce" that tasted like sweet peppers. Another very traditional food that we were served was called flija. It is a type of bread, which resembles thick crepes, stacked one on top of the other, but stickier and saltier. Jessica and I first had flija in the Zenuni household and we tasted it with Canadian maple syrup, a gift to the hosts. It truly was a mixture of two traditional cultures at that point, which was not very much appreciated by the Kosovars. Generally Kosovar food was delicious, a bit on the salty side, but thoroughly enjoyable to my foreign taste buds.

Our small group of foreigners also expressed interest that week in visiting a mosque and a church, a visit offered to us by Elvira's uncle, Skandar. He first brought us to a Serbian orthodox church, which was quite old and had elaborate ornamentation on the inside. All the writings were in Serbian. This was the first time that we were able to see their script, since it was not overtly present in town. Our guide, who did not speak English, had brought along one of our Albanian friends to translate for us. This friend had never stepped inside a Christian institution before and was rather impressed by it. He would have never entered a church had we not been in the country. After pictures and some explanations about the church, we walked across town to visit the mosque that was sometimes attended by Skandar. To be honest, the mosque from the outside was nothing impressive. My thought was that churches grabbed attention much more. However, upon entry, my first impression was proven wrong. The mosque was quite impressive. There was Arabic script written all over the walls and decorative paintings. In reality, the decor was sober when compared to the Serbian church. It was however maintained much more and well attended by followers. Our group visited a few minutes before the afternoon's prayer call and we were permitted to stay to observe the procedures. It was fascinating. The prayer call blasted from the tower of the mosque, a man's voice beautifully singing in Arabic. Old men and a few younger ones flocked to the bottom level, while we remained at the top level reserved for women. The followers bowed and stood in synchronicity as they followed the imam. The whole experience is still a blur, yet it was a truly beautiful one.

Arlind, my devout host brother, discussed Islam with me during my stay. He mentioned that young men around his age often find their way back to muslim traditions. Arlind said that until recently, he had not prayed five times a day or followed all the Islamic rituals. However, he told me that after investigating some modern day research, he was convinced of the principles of Islam. For example, Muslims are to abstain from eating any form of pork. Arlind is convinced of this truth because research has proven something along the lines of pig meat being less healthy and dirtier than that of other animals. He told me that if ever he were to find a passage in the Qu'ran that did not make sense, meaning it was not the word of Allah, he would cease to believe so firmly in Islam. Arlind had strong traditional views. As mentioned, he strongly believed in specific gender roles. Something he emphasized while speaking to me was that once married, his wife should call him "husband" and never again by his given name. Also, rarely would he be seen helping around the house. As the eldest male child, he was entitled to preferential treatment. To Arlind, women are to support their husbands and raise their children. This way of thinking highly offended me most of the time. However, he was very open in discussing differences between my atheist Canadian beliefs and his Islamic Albanian beliefs.

During our first weekend in Kosovo, our group went out to a club to party. I was surprised that nightclubs would be a thing in Kosovo considering it is a Muslim country. However, the Muslims of the Republic of Kosovo are moderate and few practice all the customs of Islam. Since the country is indeed Islamic, the experience of a nightclub was very different than that of a night out in Canada. There was no dance floor where people get inappropriately close, few people drink and being drunk is seen in a very negative light. People stick to their groups, there is no cat-calling or grabbing. The whole experience is rather tame. As in many Canadian clubs, there happened to be an altercation between a couple of guys. This was a big deal for the majority of Kosovars. A fight meant that there was probably too much alcohol, of course, but there was also a risk of there being guns nearby. Our friends told us that it was not so rare that a gun would be used or found. These weapons are the residues of the war. After the second altercation broke out that night, it was time for us to leave the party. Tension was too high and so were stress levels.

The remainder of the weekend was spent travelling throughout Kosovo, visiting sites of importance and of interest. We began by a stop at a touristic site for Kosovars and of other people from the Balkan region: the Gadime Cave. We went into the cave and walked through underground passageways. Our guide explained the history and peculiarities of the geological formations. We also made a wish in a water-filled natural formation with our Canadian currency, leaving a little souvenir of our passing. Our stay lasted a short period and we were off to our next location.

The Jashari memorial site is one of the places that marked my visit to Kosovo the most. As a huge attraction for Albanians, it was naturally packed. It remained however a very emotional experience for me. The Jasharis were an Albanian family, which was part of the Kosovo Liberation Army (KLA), and it was almost completely exterminated during the Kosovo

War. In March 1998, the village of Prezak in Drenica, where the Jasharis resided, was attacked by Serbian forces. This was not the only siege on the Jasharis and their neighbours, the first happening in 1991. The final battle between the Jasharis and the Serbs began on March 5th, 1998 and lasted four days. During the battle, all those who could fight did so, all the while Adem Jashari, the commander of the KLA, sang to encourage his family members. Fifty-three Albanians were killed during this battle in the Jashari house. Only a young girl, named Besarta, survived. She was captured by the Serbs and used to identify each body. The bodies of these Kosovar martyrs for independence are buried at a memorial site in the village of Prezak. Our group visited the burial site, which was guarded by a few soldiers who were specifically watching over Adem Jashari's grave. The Jasharis are heroes in Kosovo. The house is intact, as if the battle had happened only yesterday. There are bullet holes and signs of fire and explosions visible throughout the house. Children on educational trips were running around, laughing and screaming. The solemnity that I felt was due to the fact that I was overwhelmed by the idea that such a large number of people had died, so recently, for their country. Children as young as 5 years old had died with their parents, trying to win a better future for their fellow Albanians. These thoughts brought tears to my eyes, especially knowing about little Besarta who survived. It was an important visit for me since it opened up my eyes to some of the realities that Albanian Kosovars went through during the war. Destruction, death and sadness were part of daily life during 1998-1999 in some parts of Kosovo and my friends had lived through these events. After knowing the Jasharis' story, a deeper understanding connected me further to Kosovo and its people.

For lunch, we stopped at one of the most scenic attraction of Kosovo: Rugova Gorge. Named as the first president of Kosovo, this place is in the mountains near the Albanian border. Rugova Gorge is simply a natural wonder of the country with its waterfalls, green mountains and high rock facades. Down below the street level, there was a river in which we enjoyed a moment after our meal. The water was freezing cold, stepping in it and from rock to rock was quite the challenge. This stop was a relaxing moment, meant to uplift our spirits after the heavy visit to the Jashari house. The moment spent in Rugova Gorge also brings back special memories from my time in Kosovo.

An impromptu stop was demanded by us, the foreigners, since we had heard so much about the town we were travelling through. Krusha e Madhe is one the of success stories that emerged from the Kosovo War. This village was one of the most devastated ones during the conflict. Over 90% of all males found in Krusha e Madhe were executed and then raped by Serbian forces in 1999. Only women and children too young to gender-identify were spared. This meant that the women and young children were left behind to mourn, pick up the pieces, and rebuild. These strong women survived because they knew that their children needed them, it was for them that they worked so hard. They started a successful agriculture co-op that grows peppers and sell their products in grocery stores all over Kosovo. The women of Krusha e Madhe started their business by selling to individuals, then to grocery stores and their business has been constantly expanding. The women even received aid from USAID and other organizations in the form of machines to wash and prepare the peppers. However, they also had many other burdens because they are first mothers and then business owners. They sometimes work until midnight and this is done in terrible conditions, which are in the process of being improved. The Krusha E Madhe women are now attempting to expand internationally. Unfortunately these women do not have the infrastructure and machines to export large amounts as certain companies request. It is a work in progress, developed and run solely by women who suffered great loss. These ladies are the embodiment of success and the determination to survive. They have inspired many throughout Kosovo, including myself. We stopped by and were offered a tour of their facilities. The obvious pride and hope of the women was delightful to see. Visits from non-Kosovars are not frequent and the workers were even more proud to gain recognition from people from as far away as Canada and Japan. It was a true honour to visit Krusha e Madhe.

We ended our tour of Kosovo by stopping in the southern city of Prizren. It was a lovely town with cobblestone streets and many historical buildings, including castles, mosques and churches. Prizren is a lovely town where we stopped for a coffee along the side of the river, which was overstepped by old stone bridges. This town had a distinctly touristic atmosphere to it. Maybe it was the cleanliness or the natural beauty of the location that gave us that impression. We walked around for a while, exploring small streets and shops. As the light declined, it was time to return home to Gjilan.

The following week we had school occasionally, yet a vast amount of our time was spent in the capital, Prishtina. That week we had official meeting with members of the Kosovo parliament. These meetings mostly had as goals to promote the program, to give it exposure, and to introduce us foreigners as ambassadors for our respective countries. Dressed in our most formal attire, we attended the appointments with as much calm as we could muster. The first meeting was with the Speaker of the House, Jakup Krasniqi. This man is very important in the government of Kosovo and took a moment of his valuable time to address our group of students. He explained in broad strokes the history of Kosovo, leading up to the war in 1998-1999 and then ended with a small discussion of the current situation. News reporters and photographers were present to immortalize the moment. The media was definitely something new to me, yet it would become almost typical during our stay in Kosovo.

The same day we visited both the Deputy Minister of Culture, Youth and Sports, as well as the Deputy Minister of Internal Affairs. Both ministers discussed current issues they were working on and spoke optimistically of the future lying before Kosovo. Hajdin Abazi, the Deputy Minister of Culture, spoke especially of the problems with Kosovo's recognition in relation to sports on the international scene. Kosovars may not participate in such things as FIFA or the Olympics, since the country is not part of the United Nations as a formally recognized state. This recently caused problems for one of their athletes, a female judoka, during the Olympics who was barely allowed to participate as a member of the delegation from Albania. Hajdin Abazi seemed to emphasize only the superficial problems of his country.

For his part, the Deputy Minister of Internal Affairs, Izmi Zeka, spoke of the problems regarding the northern region of Kosovo. In the area of Mitrovica, there is little or no control over all aspects of governance. There is violence between the Albanians and Serbs, the borders are open to illegal trade, as well as many other issues. Izmi Zeka briefly touched upon these topics, yet mostly emphasized the hopeful outlook for Kosovo and for the government's improvement of its reach. We had coffee with this man and his aides, yet, to be completely honest, Zeka had a certain air of sleaziness to him. He was charismatic to be sure. Unfortunately, his charisma did not arouse any positive feelings in me. Zeka asked us mostly about our preconceptions about the country and about the image that Kosovo projects. When compared to the Deputy Minister of Culture, after the meeting with Izmi Zeka there was a distinct feeling of uneasiness felt throughout my body. He did not make me truly believe in the future of Kosovo.

Our meetings done for the day, we asked if we could wander around Prishtina a little bit. At our request, Professor Bislimi brought us to the impressive Cathedral of Blessed Mother Theresa that is being built in the capital. Although not Islamic, as the majority of Kosovars are, one cannot deny that this church is remarkable. Still under construction, most of the interior was not finished. However, the sheer immensity of the space was enough to inspire awe. On the other hand, it was odd that we could simply walk onto such a large construction site without any guide or granted access. We walked in behind the altar and had an amazing view of the entire stone structure. The construction of the Roman Catholic cathedral was commissioned by the government of Kosovo and the foundation was actually first laid down by a Muslim. There is most definitely religious tolerance in Kosovo.

We also met the mayor of Gjilan, Qemajl Mustafa, during one of our meetings during that same week. He invited us to a reception where we watched a movie about Gjilan and were the mayor discussed the possibilities for youth. He was a lovely man, positive but quite realistic as well, which I appreciated immensely. Qemajl Mustafa described Kosovo as a country with a particular culture, immense hospitality, and a very interesting position as a new state that is slowly but surely moving forward alongside various world countries. The mayor gave us an overview of the situation of Kosovo, and of Gjilan. He explained to us that approximately 40,000 students graduate from high school every year and about half of them continue studying at higher levels. However, there are only about 15,000 new jobs produced every year, which leaves 5,000 people unemployed. This has been happening since the 1990s, he said. These statistics explain the 45% unemployment rate found within the country. However, Mustafa also emphasized the fact that more and more Kosovar students are learning foreign languages and are going to school in other countries, thereby offering new possibilities for themselves and for Kosovo. However, this was not a reality that I had encountered because it was difficult and rare to cross a person on the street who speaks English. Yet it is a new trend among the youth, who do make up the majority of the population of Kosovo. Mayor Qemajl Mustafa was very open to foreign investment in Gjilan as well, yet this is also something that is not found in Kosovo since it is mostly considered to be a dangerous zone. Being very generous and welcoming, the mayor of Gjilan then invited us all out to dinner at the fanciest restaurant in town.

Our entire week was very busy indeed because in the next days we also met with the President of Kosovo, Atifete Jahjaga. As a female leader in a Muslim country, I was very impressed. Although she was exhausted having arrived in the middle of the night from a meeting abroad, President Jahjaga consented to seeing us anyway. She looked completely worn out, but welcomed us for a short period and spoke to us in impeccable English. Her speech was brief, and we could not ask any question that we had prepared amongst ourselves, yet I was quite satisfied with our visit. She agreed to a picture session, for the press and for our own pleasure, in which she grabbed me around the waist to get closer. I was side-hugged by a world leader. It was an absolutely amazing feeling. This meeting with the President of Kosovo further inspired me to aspire to work with world leaders in the future. Being a student of political science and international development, my encounter with President Jahjaga encouraged me to pursue a career in International Affairs.

Our last formal meeting during our stay was with the Parliament Member, Leader of the Opposition and President of the Vetevendosje! movement, Albin Kurti. This appointment was much less formal. We met in the headquarters of Vetevendosje! and it felt like an informal conference with any old activist. Kurti doesn't act quite like a politician. He emphasized that Vetevendosje! is actually a movement, not a party. This differentiation stems from his strong belief that Kosovo is in fact not independent and so cannot truly have any political parties. Although an eloquent speaker and a charismatic man, Albin Kurti would and should never be elected. His views are negative towards Kosovo. Since Kurti considers that there are too many barriers for true freedom and success to be achieved in Kosovo, he would not act as though the country was in fact exactly that— a country. International interference, in the form of EU assisted governance for example, is a big problem in the eyes of the leader of Vetevendosje! Kurti also mentioned a point that stuck to me quite a bit. He said that the NATO mission of KFOR in Kosovo is not stationed in order to rid the country of conflict and bring about peace, but is present with the objective of preventing another conflict from arising. It is simply stalling the beginning of a new violence, due to the ever-present elements required to spark another conflict. Albin Kurti's words echoed what some of fellow exchange students and I had already discussed. We felt like the ingredients for more fighting were present, yet none of the politicians had mentioned this to us to date. Listening to Kurti, although not an uplifting experience, felt like the truth was finally being spoken to us.

Kurti was also asked a question about the education system in Kosovo. His response to this matter was shocking to the Albanian students who were present with us. Albin Kurti told us that he believed that the large amount of private universities in Kosovo were only useful in pumping out certificates, which have no real educational value behind them. We Canadians felt this was true for the most part, having seen some of the mathematics homework that our hosts had been working on. It was the difficulty of my eighth-grade homework. However, this comment was taken differently by the Albanian students. They all attend a private university and obviously did not appreciate being told their certificates would have no value. The change in their expressions was evident to all. This was a severe lack of tact on the part of the Vetevendosje! leader. When I asked my host Adelina how she felt about Albin Kurti, her response was not positive. She told me that he was too negative, did not believe in Kosovo and that the general public did not like him. I did not find this very hard to believe. People do not wish to be told the truth in such a crude manner, politicians must be optimistic to sell their product. All the other officials we had met had done exactly that. Meeting Albin Kurti had felt like a breath of fresh air, yet more in the form of a chilling gust.

This second week of official appointments ended with a final day of class on the Friday and then a relaxing afternoon. When I attempted to isolate myself and read due to my natural tendency towards solitude, my neighbours and hosts would come speak to me in no time. It was almost as if it were not natural for people to wish to be alone in Kosovar society, which is so axed upon family and community ties. Often, I would be asked if I was okay and if I needed something. Relaxing in Kosovo was rarely done by reading a book alone for the sake of pleasure.

The next day our group of Canadians and the single Japanese student departed for a four day trip in the Balkan region, visiting Montenegro, Albania and Macedonia. We arose very early so as to get the most out of our first day. Halit, Professor Bislimi's father, joined us on our travels, so did our driver and guide Halil. Cramped into an SUV, all seven of us experienced the thrill of going through four countries together in so little time. We first drove for a few hours non-stop and had the pleasure of seeing the Kosovar and Albanian landscapes. Mountain after snowy-top mountain passed before our eyes. More often than not, when turning a corner my breath would be taken away by the beauty of what was before me. Words cannot do justice to the natural wonders of the Balkan region. Nor can they do justice to the blazing heat that accompanied us during our excursion outside of Kosovo.

We first arrived in the city of Shkodra in Albania. We stopped for a quick lunch and directed ourselves to the Castle of Shkodra. It was a wonderful structure dating all the way back to the 5th century. Unfortunately, we received no further information about the history of the castle. The view from the top of the walls was absolutely awe-inspiring. We could see the twisting rivers, a grand lake and the entire city of Shkodra from the top of the hill where the castle was situated. Agricultural fields of various hues of green, a faint haze of clouds, impressive mountains a short distance away, and ancient vestiges of the past made the view absolutely picturesque. As a scenic stop, it was simply fantastic. We could have stayed in Shkodra for a much longer period than we did, yet we had to press on to Montenegro if we wished to arrive before nightfall.

I might mention that during this part of our travels, we developed a system to rate bathrooms. We created this system due to the amount of facilities that were disgusting. Many toilets, in Kosovo and elsewhere, were simply holes in the ground where it was necessary to squat in order to do your business. If this wasn't bad enough in itself, toilet paper was rare and cleanliness was as minimal as I have ever seen. Going to the bathroom was always an adventure when on the road. If you believe that gas stations in Canada are disgusting, you have not seen anything yet. My entire perspective and expectations about bathroom facilities have completely changed since my travels in the Balkans.

We crossed the Albania-Montenegro border in the mid afternoon and headed towards the town of Ulcinj, located on the coast of the Adriatic Sea. Ulcinj is a very touristic town with few real sites to see. The Castle of Ulcinj has been converted into restaurants and hotels, with few untouched stone walls. The view of the Adriatic was absolutely stunning however. The water was a gorgeous blue and the sky was clear, it was a perfect day for a swim. Unfortunately, my bathing suit was so far down in my luggage that I could not find it in order to take my first dip in the water. The beach was covered in locals, since the tourist season had not yet begun, and I have never seen so many sunburns in one place. It seems to be the trend to not wear sunscreen in this region because even our Kosovar friends shunned any sort of protection. Their objective was to be as dark as Africans, so they said. We stayed in Ulcinj long enough to have a meal of fish filet on the beach side during sunset. It was lovely.

We drove all the way to Durres, Albania that very evening. The drive lasted about three hours and we were getting restless. We had left our Albanian hosts to vacation on their own in Montenegro. Once we arrived in the seaside town of Durres, our group had no accommodations for the night. Finding a hotel should not have been too difficult in the low season, yet our guide was looking for a good deal. Having arrived at around 10:45, we stayed stranded on the sidewalk until 1:00 in the morning. We were exhausted, but the room was nice and we were close to the Adriatic. The next day we left Durres without seeing anything because we were headed to Kruya, an hour drive away perhaps.

In Kruja, our group finally encountered some native English speakers, as well as Dutch and Polish tourists. The Albanian town of Kruja is found 650 meters above sea-level and a drive through a wooded mountain area is necessary to reach the beautiful town. The houses are built half way up the mountain, around the Castle of Kruja. This castle is the main attraction for tourists. It was the home of the historical Albanian hero Skanderbeg and was built in the 5th century. As a strategically located structure, the view of the surrounding areas was stunning yet again. From our position at the top of the castle, we could even view the Adriatic Sea. We visited the museum dedicated to Skanderbeg and to the history of the castle. We learned that Skanderbeg is seen as the defender of the Albanian people. He defended the Albanian region against the Ottoman Empire for over two decades. Statues dedicated to Skanderbeg, mostly depicting him on his horse with his famous goat helmet, are found all across Europe.

To access Skanderbeg's castle we had to go through tourist-trap alley. There were handicrafts, cheesy objects and antiques everywhere. Merchants would call out at you so you would enter their shop or admire their stall. It was slightly overwhelming. Albanian pride was evident by the amount of red and black, as well as by the number of double-headed Albanian eagle symbols. And by the end of our walk down the street, my bag was full of all the gifts that were required for my large family.

Once we got our fill of the museum and of Kruja, our group drove back to Durres where we were given a free afternoon to do as we pleased. After eating, the first thing we all wished to do was cool off in the salty water of the Adriatic. Even though the beach and shores are quite polluted with trash, as you get farther out the water becomes highly enjoyable. We floated around in the waves for almost an hour, while paddle boats went by us. In Durres, there are many tourists during high season. So the beach was set up with this purpose in mind, parasols and reclining chairs everywhere and kids attempting to rip you off. It was a typical resort town. However, the water was warm, the sun was shining and even paying for a spot to put my towel could not bring me down! Jessica and I even treated ourselves to the pleasure of having a cold beer on a pier in the Adriatic Sea. That afternoon was bliss.

At night we went to visit the Old City of Durres and the Roman Amphitheatre. This was a disappointing excursion to say the least. The amphitheatre was surrounded by a large fence, pitch-black, and badly maintained. It was located in the middle of town, but had you not known there was something there you would never notice it. One would think that such an important part of history would be better preserved. We Canadians were not impressed. Since there was not much to see, we walked around a little bit. Sadly enough, we were often stopped by beggars asking for money for their children. They were much too insistent and had no shame compared to the Kosovars who needed money. There was definitely a difference in culture between Albania and Kosovo. In Kosovo people were friendlier and more welcoming than in Albania where they people are intent on doing business no matter what. It made me realize how much more comfortable I felt in Kosovo. It was like home.

The next day we left Durres and travelled to the Albanian city of Berat. This town is now a UNESCO World Heritage Site due to the historical significance of its castle. Stunning views are not rare in Albania and Berat was no exception. From the top of the castle, where we could walk on the ruins of the walls, we had a fantastic view of the entire landscape. The sad thing about Berat was that it has only recently become a protected UNESCO site and so there are still many issues with the castle. For one thing, many Albanians have made the castle their home and so at any turn you could end up in somebody's front yard or house. This fact took away from the natural beauty of the structure since there were antennas interrupting the view and electrical wires running through and above the cobblestone street. Also, the castle was generally poorly maintained in general. It was sad to behold such a piece of history in such a dreadful state of decay. Berat is still a work in progress. However, the pictures that I took in Berat are still some of my favourites from my trip.

After departing from Berat we backtracked in order to head towards Macedonia, the last country on our four-day excursion. The landscape that we drove through got even better that day. In order to get to our next destination, Oher Lake, we needed to go through mountains from which, once at the top, you glimpse a view of the entire valley being left behind. This was nothing compared to what awaited us on the other side. Oher Lake is the most stunning natural feature that I have ever witnessed. The highest lake in Europe, Oher Lake shares its waters between both the country of Albania and that of Macedonia. The huge water mass is of the deepest blue and the mountain range frames the lake so beautifully. It was overwhelming, as if this could not be a part of reality. Words simply cannot begin to explain how magnificent the view was. We had to stop in order to seize the moment in photographs, but still the memory remains a million times better than a picture. As we travelled towards the Albanian city of Pogradeç, my eyes never left the water.

Pogradeç is a beautiful small town on the shores of Oher Lake. We begged to stay in a nice hotel beside the water and succeeded in convincing Halit. That night, we had locally-made beer and food on the shores of Oher Lake and it was fantastic. We also walked down the boardwalk of Pogradec with all the locals. On the beach there were rows of little boats in bright colours and children running around carnival attractions. The air was warm and small waves were crashing along the beach and so I took my sweet time while I walked, soaking in the moment.

Our short trip ended the next day with a stop in Macedonia. We first had a short stay in Ohrid, on the other side of Oher Lake. Macedonia was much more tourist-friendly in the sense that it was cleaner, English was spoken more frequently and there was a large variety of things to do. Jessica and I walked around together and had quite an experience. In the marketplace, we saw a shoe vendor who had the nicest hand-woven leather shoes. This old man did not speak any English nor any Albanian, with which we could have managed. He only spoke Macedonian. Beyond all that, we had none of the local currency, Macedonian denars, only euros. In order to successfully buy our pairs of shoes, we had to bargain without words and without the appropriate money. Resourceful as we are, Jessica and I managed to do this by writing down numbers related to shoe size and to the price we were willing to pay on a sheet of paper. Ohrid left me with the realization that I could manage to make it anywhere.

The capital of Macedonia, Skopje, is a very cosmopolitan and modern city. Mostly under construction, the center of Skopje was clearly being shaped to create a Macedonian identity. There were statues of historical figures and of people of importance to the country being erected. These included Alexander the Great, Skanderbeg and religious leaders. Halil, our driver and guide, had a certain disdain for Macedonian identity. He said that Macedonia is stealing from other cultures and histories, for example by displaying a statue of the Albanian hero in the center of their town, as well as by making ancient Greek history their own. This did not seem justified to me since these cultures have indeed shared many parts of their past together. However, one distinctly Macedonian claim to fame is that it is the birthplace of the famous Mother Theresa. In what is now the main square, there are golden markers showing the location of her house and a plaque commemorating it. A short distance away there is also a memorial house dedicated to Mother Theresa. In this building there is a chapel that is used a few times a week, which has glass walls that reflect the light all over, as well as a museum devoted to the life of the saint. Christianity is more openly appreciated and practiced in Macedonia than in Kosovo, that is for sure.

Our return to Kosovo was highly anticipated by our hosts and ourselves. That last week we did very little activity-wise. For me it was more about enjoying the last moments with my host family, playing soccer with our neighbours/cousins and just relaxing. One day however we were asked to attend the recording of a talk show, on which we were supposed to have a guest appearance! We received so much media attention during these three weeks, it was really unexpected. At the television show, we were each interviewed about our experience in Kosovo. My response emphasized my emotional connection to the country and its people. I also mentioned how hopeful it made me to see that most of the Kosovar politicians were optimistic for the country and improvements for the future. It was a truthful, yet diplomatic attempt to not say anything negative about Kosovo on a local television program. Nobody needs to be told that their home does not look as good as they believe, especially from the point of view of an outsider.

In my opinion, what Kosovo needs is something to export since they import about 90% of all their products. This is a huge amount of money dedicated to imports. My host brother Arlind once told me that Kosovars imported so much because they are rich. This is not the case. For a country with such an abundance of natural resources and a high percentage of the population unemployed, these resources are not utilized at all. The infrastructure is not present however. After the communist era, most factories were abandoned and the war also destroyed most of what little infrastructure remained. Now there is no money to spend on building up the proper infrastructure, be it from the government or even privately. Something that Kosovo needs desperately to push it forward is foreign investment. It would be more than necessary, but with an international image that is far from positive, this will not soon happen. International presence in a country means it is not stable and that there is still a chance of conflict. This is something that investors see and it stops them from profiting from Kosovo. Life in Kosovo is not that expensive. Shirts can easily be bought for 1 euro and bread for a little as 40 cents or ten tomatoes for just as much. With an idle young workforce and the cost of living being lower than the average European country, investors could do well in business in Kosovo and it would profit the country at the same time. It is a matter of changing the preconceived ideas towards Kosovo. This is something that we were often questioned about: our thoughts about Kosovo before we travelled to the state. Thinking back at this, I too was wrong about my perception of Kosovo. The problem is that most people will not investigate further.

As fantastic as my experience in Kosovo was, there were many moments that I found difficult. An example of this was witnessing the innumerable amount of pictures of missing friends and family members that have been displayed along the fence of the parliament building in Pristina. These photographs of the young and the old act as a plea for justice. Albanian Kosovars want closure from events that happened over 13 years ago, which will only be brought by the certainty that these loved ones are indeed dead and not captured by Serbian forces. It was hard to imagine what so many people, including my friends, went through. Adelina and her family went to live in Macedonia during the war, whereas Alban, Gordie's host, slept in a bunker with over forty other people every night. Halit Bislimi spoke to us about his experience during the war when he was forced to stay in the country. He had buried photographs and memories in his backyard in order to have something from his previous life if ever his home was destroyed. His son, Faton Bislimi, left the country for Macedonia during the war and Halit was not sure if he would ever see him again. While he told us these things, he began to cry. It was these types of stories, coming from people whom I learned to care about and appreciate immensely, that broke my heart. Yet, it was also these stories that made me feel connected to the Albanian history in Kosovo. The people were willing to share their personal stories and lives with me during my stay, I was not expecting to receive so much from a people who have been through such hardships. Kosovo opened its heart to me. I witnessed its beauty, its horror and its hope. Kosovars are statistically the most optimistic individuals in Europe and I wholeheartedly believe that these numbers are not lying.

The Balkans Peace Program brought us to Kosovo so we could understand the reality of the country. We were introduced to its history, its culture and its society. The reality of Kosovo is quite different than what the average citizen of the world may think. There is beauty, no fighting in the peaceful areas, the people are welcoming and have great expectations for their country's future. One of the girls that I met in Arlind's English class, named Donjetë, best expressed this hope me to.

When I mentioned my desire to eventually do a Master's degree in Europe, she said that she wished she could suggest Kosovo and that eventually she hoped her country would be a place where someone like me would wish to visit, maybe even study. In that simple statement her expectations for her country were obvious. Another girl that I met, Farije, impressed me maybe the most. Farije studies international business at the University of Prishtina, the state university. I met her only twice, but she left quite an impression on me and Jessica as well. When she discussed her aspirations for her country and how she wanted to contribute, Farije inspired me. She had one of those particular personalities, the ones that make you believe in the future. Farije and Donjetë are but two examples of the youth of Kosovo expressing their optimism. The younger generation of Kosovo will undoubtedly push the country in the right direction. The will is certainly there.

After this experience, not only has my understanding of Kosovo increased, but my appreciation for a people who have survived through so much increased tenfold. International assistance has been given to the Kosovars, but it is their resilience that has made them survivors. Success for this country will begin from within. A small example of this is Krusha e Madhe's women and their triumph after great loss. Kosovo really transformed who I am and how I perceive the world. My desire to help others has been reinforced by this one-of-a-kind experience. I have promised my Kosovar friends that I would come back someday and I would do so in a heartbeat.

CHAPTER 4

Kosovo—An Unforgettable Experience

Masayuki Kishimoto

TO GO TO KOSOVO was one of the best decisions that I have ever made in my life. I am confident that I learned a lot while being involved in the Balkans Peace Program, which benefits me in many aspects. I totally understand the reason why my friends get jealous of me when I talk about my unique experiences in this program. I was extremely lucky to meet with those who made me feel like I was a part of their family, which I really appreciate. The three weeks when I was involved in this program passed so quickly, it seems like it just happened. Overall, it was fortunate for me to learn an interesting topic like post-conflict development from the great professor who kept me interested in the topic and with my hospitable classmates with whom I shared wonderful experiences. Therefore, my summer in 2012 became awesome because of the wonderful memories and experiences in this program. I truly appreciate the warm support from those who gave me such a precious experience.

To begin with, I had a strong feeling that I wanted to go to the Balkan countries, starting from the time I began studying world history in high school. The more I studied the history of the Balkan countries, the more I was attracted and motivated to keep studying, and the more I became interested in the global world. Since then, my feeling toward going abroad had become greater and greater. And now, I am in the second year of my studying at one of the Canadian universities. I am having such a wonderful time now. If I had not studied Balkan history, I would not have been in Canada. Moreover, I would not have had a chance to go to Kosovo. My Canadian university gave me a chance to participate in the Balkans Peace Program.

Before I am going to talk about my experience in Kosovo, I would like to mention my appreciation to my family who positively supported me to go to Kosovo.

Before the Class Started

Even though I was truthfully excited after I applied for this program, I was a little bit nervous because I had not been informed about who was coming to the Prishtina Airport to pick me up and who my host family would be. Since I wanted to bring some souvenirs for my host family, I wanted to know a little about them. Except for the information about who was supposed to pick up the exchange students from Canada and Japan at the airport, I think this program was well-organized. However, I was excited rather than nervous when I left Japan for Kosovo.

I had not had any problems from the time I applied for this program to when I arrived at Prishtina Airport. I did have trouble in that my luggage was delayed when I arrived at the airport in Prishtina. After a long overnight flight from Osaka,

Japan via Istanbul in Turkey, I was really tired. I just wanted to get my luggage and pass through customs. However, my luggage never came out, but those who took the same flight as I did started leaving one by one as they picked up their luggage. Finally, I became alone but still I had not gotten my luggage, which made me even more tired. I kept waiting for my luggage for more than 10 minutes, but no baggage similar to mine came out. So, I went to the customer service office to ask if my luggage had been sent to Prishtina from Istanbul. I was told that there was no information regarding my luggage, and that I should call the office the following day to make sure if my luggage arrived. Since I was supposed to be picked up at the exit of the airport, I had to go without my luggage and started walking toward the exit. On the way to the exit, I was stopped by a security officer in front of the gate. The security officer suspiciously looked at me and asked me a lot of questions such as: what were the purposes of my visiting, where I was going to stay, where I was from and so on. I responded to security that I came to Kosovo to study the post-conflicts developments at Gjilani University College, and I was from Japan. Still, the security officer seemed to be suspicious and asked me to show my passport. After the security officer saw my passport, he looked even more suspicious of me because I took my passport picture two years ago, which I do not think looks like I do today. He asked other security people if they thought that my passport photo looked like me. They nodded and made a gesture to let me pass the gate to the exit. I was super tired by the time I met my host brother who was supposed to pick me up at the exit of the airport

When I passed the exit gate, everyone started looking at me, which made me feel like I was a celebrity. As I was going out from the exit gate, I found a guy who had a white paper with a name, but it was not mine. Since I noticed that he was not the guy who was supposed to pick me up and did not look at him, it was kind of the guy to come to me to make sure if I was not the person on the white paper. When I found two guys, one of whom had a paper with my name, I was so happy and relieved. After greetings, I told them that I lost my luggage and I had to call the customer service office the following day. Since we had to wait for another exchange student coming soon, they took me to an office where missing luggage was stored to double-check if my luggage was there, but there was nothing similar to mine. I was really disappointed because I thought that I would be fine somehow. By the way, my first impression of Kosovo was that there were so many beautiful women. Thus, I would say that I was excited rather than disappointed.

On the way to Gjilani, we took a break to have something to drink at the tallest building in Prishtina. Since the view from there was awesome, I got excited and recovered from the long flight and the luggage delay. I was curious about everything I saw since I arrived at the airport. Of course, the city view was impressive, but what I was most interested about was the size of the small macchiato. It was the smallest coffee cup that I had ever had. When I saw the small cup of macchiato, I honestly thought it was a joke because it was as large as a ping pong ball.

In this program, what I liked and enjoyed the most was that I had a lot of free time to hang out with my classmates and their friends because I wanted to meet as many people as I could.

By the time when I met my host family, I was hungry because I only had a small cup of macchiato that day. After I told them that I wanted to get something to eat, they took me to the restaurant in front of Gjilani University College. However, I did not know what food would be good to eat, so I ordered the same meal as my host brother did. What surprised me was that I did not get a glass of water. In Japan or Canada, I have usually been served a glass of water as I order something. Therefore, I assumed that I would get a glass of water as well. Then, I asked for some water. However, I got a large bottle of water, which was really surprising to me. To be honest, I did not need this much water, but I did not know how to say that I did not want to have this in Albanian. Thus, I decided to get the water. However, it was a good thing that I did not return the water. It was what I actually needed because what I ordered was too salty for me. In general, I found it that food in Kosovo was either too salty or too sweet for me.

I had met a lot of cousins of my host brothers and sister. As I went back home from the restaurant, I met one of their cousins. He suggested me to take a walk with him around the city of Gjilan. Since I was not really tired any more, I went out with them. I had a good time with them. They bought me something like seeds and showed me how to eat them because they told me that I had to use my teeth. However, it was really difficult for me. While I was struggling to figure out how to eat the seeds smoothly, they came up an idea that we were going to meet a beautician, and then asked me to kiss her cheek after saying " I love you" in Albanian. When I did what they told me to do, the beautician handled what I did to her in a way that we all could get a good laugh. At that time, I thought I could get along well with those who I was going to meet in Gjilan somehow.

In addition, he asked me to go for drink to one of the most famous restaurants in Gjilan. Even though I was still stuffed from what I had at the restaurant, I wanted to go out and spend my time with them. I was glad that I went out: It was a unique experience for me to have macchiato at the exotic restaurant like Bujana. While chatting with him, he told me that he has a lot of cousins: so many that he did not even know how many cousins he has. I was a little bit jealous of him because I do not have any cousins. By the way, I am pretty sure that none of my Japanese friends have more than thirty cousins.

Before we went home, we also went to a bar to try local beers in Gjilan. I had a bottle of beer, Peja, which I found great and tasty and I loved it. However, I did not enjoy the smoky atmosphere at the bar even though the beer was great. Like Japanese restaurants, I wanted the bar to have two separate places for smoking people and non-smoking people because I hoped to avoid second-hand smoke when I was eating or drinking. What I was surprised at was that some tobacco sellers came into the bar and sold tobacco without checking any identification.

As we went back home, it was kind of him to take me to his house to give me some traditional foods and Turkish coffee. I liked the traditional food, but not the Turkish coffee to be honest because I did not enjoy the bitterness: it was the bitterest coffee that I have ever had. Since I did not put any sugar in the coffee, I felt like I was drinking mud. Since I had told them that I did not like adding sugar into tea, they did not suggest to me to put sugar in the coffee. As I was making a face, he and his family laughed at how I reacted. I tried to finish the Turkish coffee, but I could not although I added two cups of sugar. It would have been great if I had put more sugar into the coffee. However, I did not want to put any more sugar because I thought I would feel sick if I put in further additional sugar.

My first day in Kosovo was a long, but a great day: I had a lot of fun.

The next day, I finally got my luggage back. When my host brother took a phone call that my luggage had arrived at Prishitina Airport, I was relieved even though I had to go to the Airport to pick my luggage up because they would not deliver it to me. A security lady asked me to open it to make sure if all my stuff was not stolen or broken as I got my luggage back. I worried if somebody opened it and touched my stuff, but there was nothing wrong: I was truthfully relieved.

When I went back to Gjilan, my host brother told me that we were going to meet my classmates who would study with us for three weeks, beginning the following day: I was really excited to meet them. It was a wonderful time to get to know each other. However, I could not remember all of their names at once. It took a while to match the individual names with their faces. Even though I could not remember all of their names, I could imagine that this program was going to succeed and be meaningful to me somehow. I looked forward to studying with them the following day, and I could not wait to go to school.

The First Two Weeks of the Course

To begin with, it was such a beneficial opportunity to study the post-conflicts development in Kosovo with those who actually experienced the war. The topic that I learned in this course was unique and interesting to me: it was also difficult and complicated. Since I had studied world history, I already had some knowledge about what happened to Kosovo in the late 90's. However, I had a little information concerning what has happened since the war ended.

When I was young, my grandparents told me their experience during the Pacific War. It was shocking and unbelievable to me. I could not imagine that I would have to escape to shelters when I was on the way to go home. When I thought about what happened to those who were at the same age as me in Kosovo, I felt sad.

As I started learning about post-conflict development, I have had a lot of time to think about myself and my own life. Since I was born, I was brought up in a safe and peaceful environment. For instance, my Japanese passport. It is relatively easy for me to go abroad because I do not have to take visas. I have been to many places such as Canada, the United States, France, Kosovo, Albania, Montenegro and Macedonia without visas: I have not had any problems so far. Therefore, I felt it was unfair to my classmates when they told me that it was hard for them to get visas to go abroad, except the near countries such as Albania. By hearing their story, I thought to myself that I should appreciate all who supported and gave me a chance to go or study abroad.

It was a unique experience to go to some religious places in Gjilan such as the Serbian Orthodox Church and a mosque in Gjilan. The ornaments in both places were cool, gorgeous and beautiful. If I had not participated in this program, I would not have been able to go into these religious places. I appreciated all who gave us an opportunity to go into the religious places and look around inside the buildings.

I enjoyed visiting many places in Gjilan, especially Vali Ranch. There were many animals such as horses, carps, peacocks and more. It was so surprising for me to see the carps in a pond because I did not expect to see them in Kosovo. What I was excited about was spending my time where I was surrounded by white marbles with blue water like the restaurant at Vali Ranch, which I had always wanted to do because it looked so exotic. Since the weather was not good, we decided to stay inside the building where there were no white marbles; I wished I could have had drinks outside.

Great Opportunities to Meet the Greatly Important Persons in Kosovo

I was extremely excited to meet the important persons in Kosovo. I thought it would be a wonderful opportunity for me to learn something from them such as the way they spoke and listened to us. My first impression when I met them at first time was that they looked hospitable and friendly. What I learned from them was that it is important to make people feel comfortable when greeting them in the first place by smiling and being polite to everybody.

Connection between Japan and Kosovo

On the 6th of June 2012, the prime minister of the Republic of Kosovo met with Hiroyuki Ishige, President of Japan External Trade Organization. "At this meeting, they discussed on furthering the economic development between the two countries and the investment opportunities the Republic of Kosovo offers to foreign investors" (Republika E Kosoves, 2012). I was glad and happy with the fact that both Japan and Kosovo were trying to build a stronger bond between the two countries. I hope both business people from Japan and Kosovo will consider more business with each other so that they will develop a deeper connection and a greater relationship. When I heard many buses in the city of Prishtina were manufactured and given by Japanese manufacture companies, I was glad. While I lived in Kosovo for three weeks, I had never felt unsafe. In addition, I found out that people in Kosovo were hospitable so that there would be more opportunities for Japanese businesses in Kosovo.

At that evening, my host father told me that the news on television was about when the prime minister of the Republic of

Kosovo visited Japan: I was excited to see it. Even though I did not understand what the announcer was broadcasting then, I was glad to see the heads of our countries together on television.

Media Experiences

Some of the most impressive memorial moments I had in this program were the media experiences such as being in newspapers and being on television in Kosovo. What I enjoyed the most was to be on television. Even though I have been on television a couple of times in Japan, I was nervous because I had to speak my second language, English. Yet, once the recording started, I was not nervous at all, but I was excited to get interviewed. I naturally readied myself somehow as the recoding was carrying on. However, the longer I stayed in the recording place, the hotter it got. By the time my speaking turn came, I was extremely hot. Since I was the last one to be interviewed among the five international students, I had to wait for like an hour in what felt like a sauna. I was super exhausted before my turn came to be interviewed.

In general, I thought I did a good job with the interviews in English. The more I spoke, the more comfortable I became, and I felt confident to be interviewed and discuss my experience in this program. Everything seemed to be going perfectly until the reporter asked me to say something in my language, Japanese.

Since I did not expect that I would speak about anything in Japanese, I suddenly got nervous because I did not know what to say. Speaking in my second language was more comfortable than my first language: that was a weird experience for me. Anyway, I just said that I was hungry and I would like to get something to eat. If it had not been in Kosovo, what I said then would have not been on television: It was totally nonsense. I should have had something funny to say.

There are three memorable experiences which I really enjoyed: working out at a gym, travelling around the Balkan countries and communicating with those who I met in this program.

Working out at a Gym

The reason why working out at a gym was one of my memorable experiences was that it was totally different from how I had usually worked out at a gym in Canada or Japan: They worked out to be bodybuilders. It was a beautiful sunny day: It was extremely hot day which made me feel like staying home. However, I decided to go to the gym with them since I had not worked out since I had come to Kosovo. I went to a gym in Gjilan with two of my classmates who are one year younger than me. On the way to go to the gym, I saw many junior high school students. As I expected, they stared at me and said something in

Albanian. I assumed that it must be a rare experience for them to see Japanese people in Gjilan and I was probably the first Japanese whom they encountered in their life, which I liked.

As soon as I saw those who were training at the gym, I was overwhelmed by the fact that they looked twice or three times as big as me. In addition, there were so many posters of bodybuilders looking like monsters to me. I thought to myself that this was not the place where I should be. I just wanted to do exercise to stay healthy. Yet, working out with them was fun. As I kept training with my classmates, I talked with some of the strangers who told me that I looked like Jackie Chan. Since I was often called Jackie Chan in those three weeks, I was sort of getting used to be called Jackie Chan. However, more surprisingly, the other strangers also told me that I looked like Keisuke Honda or Shinji Kagawa, who are two of the most famous Japanese soccer players. I was proud of being called someone like them, but I thought they were just saying the names of someone from Asia who they knew. Since I spent approximately two hours building up my chest with effective advice from my classmates, I suffered from severe sore chest muscles during my entire trip to the near countries.

After we worked out, we went to a supermarket to get something to drink. Since I had too much water when I was working out because my classmates told me that I should drink a lot of water when I worked out, I did not feel like drinking anything. Yet I was hungry. I saw one of my friends bought a processed chicken, and I wanted to get one as well because the chicken looked great and the classmate told me how good it was. To be honest, I really enjoyed my first and maybe my second bite. However, the more I ate, the less I enjoyed it. It was so salty that eating the processed chicken made me feel like drinking more water, which I did not want to do.

Travelling Around the Balkan Countries

I have awesome memories of watching the changing views such as magnificent valleys, beautiful beaches and historical places on our travel to Albania, Montenegro and Macedonia. Even though it was a long driving trip, I never got bored since I enjoyed the impressive views, which were totally different from what I had seen, and I always felt relaxed by the great scenes of nature. Since I did so many things in this trip, I would like to write about my experiences time by time.

The first day, we met at Gjilani University College in the very early morning. I remember that everyone did look sleepy, of course including myself. As I expected, I fell asleep as soon as we left Gjilani University College. When we were close to the border between Kosovo and Albania, I woke up because I had to show my passport. Since there were so many cars in front of us and it seemed to take a long time to get to customs, I got out of the van and stretched myself. While we were chatting and taking pictures, the cars suddenly started moving so that we had to run to catch our van: It was embarrassing for me. As our driver showed my passport to the customs officer, I worried about if the security recognized my passport photo as myself because that seems to have been a problem at the Prishitna Airport. Moreover, I did not think that many Japanese people had passed the border from Kosovo to Albania so that I might be asked many questions again. Fortunately, I could pass the border without any questions. I thought that I should travel with my friends from Kosovo when I travel around the Balkan countries again.

Shkodër

On our way to go to Shkodër in Albania, I saw a huge rock like a mountain which I had never seen. There were a lot of impressive scenes of nature such as great mountains and magnificent valleys. Someday, I would like to drive there: The road to Albania from Prizren in Kosovo was newly paved with asphalt, which was different from the ones in Gjilan. What I liked was that we could easily stop to take pictures of the wonderful views, unlike highways in Japan.

We visited Shkodër and had lunch a cozy restaurant. Since I wanted to try a Greek salad, I ordered it. Yet, I was surprised at the amount of olives, like more than twenty olives.

Since I did not want to leave food behind me, I ate all of them. Thus, all I remember was the taste of olives.

By the way, I was always the last one who got our meals during this trip. It was kind of funny for me that my salad was served later than pizza which my friends ordered: I believed that an appetizer should not be the last one to be served

After lunch, we took a walk around the pedestrian street known as Sheshi or Pjaca on Kol Idromeno Street where there was a wonderful stone pavement street between small coffee shops and souvenir shops. As I was walking the street, I saw the most beautiful sky that I have ever seen in my life. I took a lot of pictures of the beautiful sky and the exotic street, which I really enjoyed. Whenever I show these photos to my friends and tell my stories, they always become jealous. I really wish I had had the time to have a coffee break then because the circumstance made me feel like taking a break there.

On the way to our next step to a castle in Shkodër, I was dying from heat. I did not believe that it was middle of June, but it was like August. I do not think the temperature was not above 35 degrees, but the strong sunshine made me feel like it was above 40 degrees. Thus, I just hoped to get to the castle because I knew that it was located on the top of a hill where I could feel refreshing wind. Moreover, the views from the castle were amazing enough to make me forget my uncomfortable feeling of being so very hot. Unlike the Japanese historical places, I could go anywhere to touch and take pictures. Even though I sometimes felt dangerous to be there, I really liked exploring the historical place. Thus, I scaled the outer wall and took a picture with the Albanian national flag as if I was like a general. Since I was enjoying exploring the castle, I forgot the time when I was supposed to be back.

Ulcinj (Ulqin)

Since the road from Kosovo to Albania was well-maintained, I did not worry about the quality of the road from Shkodër to Ulcinj in Montenegro, yet it was not as great as the one to Albania. It was like small, tiny and winding roads in the Japanese countryside: I almost got car sick. However, I became refreshed as we arrived at Ulcinj and saw the beautiful and exotic beach. Not only the beach, but also I was impressed by the site of a castle. What I was impressed most about the site of the castle was the historical water supply. I really liked the idea that the local community living in the site of the castle shared something historical and kept using it. I would like to live with something historical which everybody in a local community share and keep using.

After visiting the site of a castle, I went down to the beautiful beach to take a relaxing break. The water there was saltier than I had ever experienced, but it was cleaner and clearer. As the sun was about to set, it was getting cold so I stopped swimming. Even though it was a short time for me to swim, I really enjoyed and relaxed.

The best part of my stay in Ulcinj was having a great dinner. It was such a good time to have dinner after swimming in view of the beautiful beach like the one in Ulcinj when the sun was about to set. Since the restaurant that we went to was in front of the beach, I expected the fish they served would be great so I ordered fish, which was fantastic. I only spent a few hours in Ulcinj, but really enjoyed the experiences, such as visiting the site of the castle, swimming in the water and having dinner in front of the beach. Ulcinj is a small town, but there are many fun things to do. After having fun in Ulcinj, I became sleepy and kept sleeping until arriving at a hotel in Durrës. My first day of the trip was long, but wonderful.

The second day, we went to Krujë to visit Muzeu Kombëtar Gjergj Kastrioti Skënderbeu (National Museum George Castrioti Scanderbeg) and came back to Durrës.

Krujë

Krujë was a different place from anywhere I have ever been, so I really liked staying there. It became one of my favourite places that I visited. Seeing the city of Krujë and the Adriatic Sea further from Muzeu Kombëtar Gjergj Kastrioti Skënderbeu was so awesome that I felt it could not be compared to anyplace. Not only the view toward the Adriatic Sea, but also the view toward the mountains behind was amazing: They were like waves on one side, and walls protecting me on the other.

It was a great opportunity to hear the history of Albania at Muzeu Kombëtar Gjergj Kastrioti Skënderbeu. In the end of the guided tour, there was a book in which those who visited Muzeu Kombëtar Gjergj Kastrioti Skënderbeu could write anything they wanted. Thus, I wrote that it was great to come visiting there, in Japanese. While I was writing the Japanese words, many people started gathering around me and were interested in watching me write. I felt like I was solving difficult mathematic problems which only I could know the way to solve.

There were many more things that I enjoyed such as shopping even though I was asked to buy something more many times. What I enjoyed most were the conversations with those who were working at the souvenir shops. When they asked me to buy some goods which I did not think that I was going to buy, I asked them how they were doing. After basic conversations like asking how they were doing, they offered me discounts. When I was shopping alone, I did not always get discounts when I was looking at goods. In contrast, when I was shopping with more people, I always got discounts when I was looking at goods. What I learned from shopping at Krujë was that it was a better idea to shop with more people, not alone.

Durrës

It was such a great decision we made that we spent one more day in Durrës. I heard that Durrës had a high reputation for the beautiful beaches, which I strongly agree with. I had always wanted to go to beautiful and splendid beaches like Durrës. As we went to the beach, a young guy came to us and asked us to pay him two Euros for two chairs and one beach parasol. Since the young guy did not wear a uniform like beach staff, I hesitated to pay him because I wondered if he was a guy who was working at the beach. There were many young people my age or younger, who seemed extremely excited. I truthfully enjoyed swimming and taking a walk along the beach. The fact that the water was warm made me feel relaxed and let me forget the time.

Since the water was getting blacker and blacker for some reason, I went up to the beach and started talking a walk. Almost all of those who I passed each other stared at me and sometimes looked back to me. By the time I was walking along the beach, I had become used to people staring at me with surprise on their faces so that I did not really mind their behaviour. However, I felt some of them were rude to me because they started saying something behind me after we passed each other. At most times, I did not understand what they said, so I did not tell them anything. On the other hand, I knew the word of Chinese in Albanian. Thus, I told them that I was not from China, but Japan, do not make a mistake in Albanian to whoever told me that I was from China. I did not mean to embarrass them, but all I wanted to do was to surprise them and see how they reacted. I really enjoyed how they reacted because all of them were surprised and closed their mouths immediately. At the same time, I wished I could speak more fluently in Albanian so that their reaction might be different.

As I kept walking along the beach, I found a tattoo stand. What I was curious about the tattoo stand was that I found a few Japanese characters and Chinese characters. Thus, I asked a tattoo artist at the tattoo stand if those Japanese characters were popular in Durrës. Then, he nodded. I was happy to see the Asian characters there since I had never expected that. However, it was a little bit sad for me that the tattoo artist did not know which characters were Japanese or Chinese. Moreover, he did not know the meaning of the Japanese and Chinese characters. Of course I was happy to see my language in Durrës, but I wanted him to know what language he was going to use for his art.

After all, it was such a refreshing break walking along the beach. After walking, I took a nap hoping to get suntanned. I was just trying to sleep for about an hour. Yet, I slept longer than I planned so that I got sunburned. The problem I had when I woke up was not the pain from sunburn, but I felt thirsty. I looked over the beach to try to find someone selling water.

Even though I could find some vendors, none of them were selling water. Therefore, I had to leave the beach to go to a convenience store for water. Once I left the beach, I did not feel like going back to the beach, so I went to my room at the hotel.

I had had a great time until dinner that night at a deserted restaurant: It was like a botanical garden. What I did not like about the restaurant was that there were so many flying insects. The longer I stayed there, the more flying insects were gathering around me. If I had not had to wait for my meal for about an hour, I could have been patient. Since it took such a long time to get my meal, I was not really happy when it finally arrived. I had just wanted to escape from the botanical restaurant as soon as I could. What was worse, the meal I had chosen was the saltiest lamb that I had ever tasted. The only thing I liked about the botanical restaurant was that I could get a bottle of beer.

Even though I did not have a good time at dinner that night, I had a great time taking a walk in the main area of Durrës. I really enjoyed taking a walk around because I liked exploring an exotic place like Durrës. What I liked were the soft orange lights because they kept me calm and relaxed, although there were noises from those who were watching a soccer game with full excitement. On the other hand what I did not find impressive was the amusement park in Durrës. It was not enjoyable to walk around inside the amusement park because many people came to ask me for money many times. I could not have time to look around. On the way back to my hotel, I had ice cream with many desserts, which was the greatest one that I had had for three weeks.

Berat

I truthfully enjoyed exploring a historical place in Berat while taking pictures. Since it was such a wonderful sunny day without clouds, I got sunburned. Since I was enjoying exploring the site of the historical place, I did not notice that I got sunburned until it really began to hurt. Overall, I had a great time visiting a unique historical place like the one in Berat. What I was excited about most was seeing the stone arched gateway. The first picture I saw when I started studying world history was the stone arched gateway. Therefore, I had always hoped to see it. Since there was a great chance of it collapsing if I stood on the edges of the stone arched gateway, I did not. However, I enjoyed walking along the edges on stone walls. The view from the top of the stone walls was amazing because I could see the historical buildings such as the stone arched gateway and the beautiful nature such as great mountains all around me.

Ballollorve

On the way to Pogradec in Albania, there was a perfect place to view amazing, beautiful and exotic scenery of

Ballollorve. I wish I could have had more time to take a break and see the wonderful view from the top of high mountains where the beauty of nature was all around me. For example I could see a wonderful view of Ballollorve when I stood looking west. On the other hand, I could see a beautiful lake view when I stood facing east. To be honest, I thought it was an ocean when I saw Lake Ohrid at first. The view of Lake Ohrid with the blue sky was so amazing that I will never forget that view.

Pogradec

As soon as I got to my room at the hotel to stay that night, I went down to the lake to swim. The water was clear, beautiful and refreshing, yet it was cold. Since it was so great to swim in the lake, it became the favourite place that I had a chance to go swimming in this program. Even though only three of us were swimming then, I really enjoyed it. However, the water got colder and colder as the sun was about to set, so I stopped swimming and went up to my room. I wish I could have had a chance to go swimming in the lake once more.

It was a great time to take a walk in Pogradec with my travelling members when the sun was about to set. Even though there were so many noisy young people, the wonderful lake view made me feel calm and relaxed. On the way back to the hotel, I was called to by a beautiful lady with her friends sitting near a fountain. Most of the times, I talked with the lady who started talking to me first. She told me that they studied at a university in the United States, and also told me that she was from Pogradec and had come back for her summer vacation. If I was from Pogradec, I would have also wanted to come back for every summer vacation. What we were talking about most was how we liked studying abroad. It was a good time to exchange our opinions of studying abroad with the lady from Pogradec. However, what I thought I should have done was to ask her number or email address because she was really beautiful as well as her friends.

I enjoyed having dinner at a restaurant in front of the hotel. To be honest, the quality of the meal I had was good, yet it was not the one I ordered. What I was more impressed about was that the waiters routinely took orders, and randomly served meals. One of them took my order, another of them got me water and others got me my meal. I assumed that the reason why they did so was that they wanted to watch a soccer game on a big screen. Rather than being disappointed, I was amused at how they treated customers.

At the Macedonian side of the lake, was one of the most beautiful views that I have ever seen. What I was impressed about most was the colour of the water which had several different colours such as green, white and blue. All I saw was the great beauty of nature, including the beautiful lakes all around me. However, there was no single way down to the beach. I wish I could have found it so that I could swim there.

Ohrid (Ohër)

I really liked walking around in the city of Ohrid in Macedonia while shopping. As I was walking, I found a beautiful fountain with a mosque behind. What I wanted to do in Ohrid was to get something for my host brother and sister. Since I wanted to buy some souvenirs for my host sister and brother, I went to many stores to look for something that I wanted to buy for them. Yet, I could not find anything that I liked.

Skopje (Shkup)

It was such a great time taking a walk in Skopje although it was pretty hot. What I liked most about Skopje was the atmosphere of the city. I liked walking on the stone pavement and looking at the monuments such as Alexander the Great. Since it was still hot, sitting at the edge of the fountain was a pleasant respite. The reason I liked the monument so much was that it seemed a place of rest and relaxation for the local people.

I was surprised at the fact that it was about thirty-nine degrees, which was the highest temperature that I have ever experienced. What I did when I was walking in Skopje was drink cold water. I could not walk around without a bottle of water: I drank 2 bottles of water within an hour. When I was having a traditional Macedonian soup, the temperature of the restaurant was even hotter than outside because the air conditioner was not powerful enough to offset the heat from the kitchen. Since the soup was great, I did not really find it was uncomfortable. However, I escaped from the restaurant as soon as I finished eating my meal.

It was sincerely surprising for me that a guy working at a local restaurant started talking to me in Japanese when I was walking on a street. He said to me "Konnichiwa", which means hello in Japanese. What surprised me most was that he could distinguish me as Japanese and started talking to me in Japanese. As we kept talking in Japanese, the local people around us seemed to be surprised and started looking at us. I really enjoyed watching their reactions. Since I was interested in the reason he could speak Japanese, I asked him where he learned to speak the language. He told me that he studied Japanese by watching Japanese anime at home. Even though it was a short conversation with him because I had to go, I was happy to talk with him in Japanese. I wish I could have had more time to talk with him.

Not only the guy, but also those who I met in Skopje seemed to be interested in speaking to me although many of them did not know how to speak Japanese. Most of the time, they just said to me "hello" while smiling at me. Therefore, it was relatively easy for me to start chatting with them so that we could exchange opinions with each other. It was such a good time to talk with the local people where I was traveling.

However, I had not met any Japanese people during my stay in the Balkan countries. It was unusual for me not to encounter any Japanese people when I was travelling.

It was such a wonderful trip and I had so much fun. When I saw sunset from Skopje Citadel, I felt sad because that amazing travel would be over soon. I appreciated to all who planned, helped and supported me to have such memorable experience in the near Balkan countries.

Communicating with those who I met on this Program

Not only visiting the historical places and seeing the great views of nature, but also hanging out with my classmates and those who I met through the Balkans Peace Program are part of my wonderful memories. All of them were such sweethearts and were always friendly to me, and were still nice to me after this program ended. I was happy that they treated me like their brother so that I always felt I was a part of their community. I always appreciated that they tried to help me have a good time whenever they had free time. For instance, they asked me to go out to have a cup of coffee. Since I wanted to spend my free time with them, I really enjoyed staying with them.

First of all, it was so lucky for me to stay with my host brother. He always drove me anywhere I asked him to go without any complaints. However, there was one thing that I did not appreciate about him: He played music so loud that I could not hear what he was saying. One day, I planned to do something to him with help from my host sister. What I did with my host sister was that I took a photo of him sleeping and set it as the screen photo of his laptop. It was unfortunate that I could not see his reaction when he saw his own sleeping face as he started his laptop: I wish I could have seen his reaction then.

Café break

It was great that I had many chances to take a break at cafeterias when I was in Gjilan. I usually ordered macchiato and sometimes ice cream called "akullore", which was nice. Since I went to cafeterias, I became confident to order what I would like to have in Albanian. The reason why I asked in Albanian was that I wanted to see the reactions of clerks: I was always excited to see the way they reacted to how I ordered. It was funny for me that they double-looked at me after I spoke Albanian.

One day, I went to Boka bar in Gjilan with my host brother and sister to make an appointment for that night. One of the clerks working at the bar had gone to Halifax in Canada during the war in Kosovo. He told me his story about when he lived in Halifax. When I showed him some of my pictures taken in Halifax, he looked happy and he told me that he still remembered what he did in Halifax. I was glad to that members of his host family there were kind, friendly and nice to him. It was nice talking with him because both of us had a great time in Halifax. We talked a lot.

That night, I went to the bar with my classmates. It was such a great time while chatting, drinking and dancing with them. What I enjoyed most was that they taught me how to dance.

Playing with neighbours' kids of my host family

I really enjoyed playing with the kids because they always came asking me to play with a big smile. There were four kids with whom I played with a lot. First, the youngest boy always came and threw a ball at me from zero distance. As soon as he pushed the ball to me, he ran away from me. He had the largest smile when he was running away. Second, the oldest girl was taking care of the rest of three kids and asked me to throw the ball into the sky as high as I could. When I threw the ball into the sky, she seemed to be excited and asked me to do more and more. Third, the oldest boy always kicked the ball far away. I was pretty sure that he was trying to make me run to get the ball. Finally, the youngest girl always come and asked me to give her the ball no matter when I had it. Even though what I was doing was always the same, I never got bored because playing with the kids was fun, and they made me forget the time. One day, I asked them to take a picture with me because they were so cute and adorable. The good thing was that they gladly nodded, The bad thing was that they never stopped, but kept moving so that I could not have a chance to talk a picture with all of them. I found it peaceful to play with the kids from the local community. Bazaar:

It was a unique experience for me to go to the bazaar in Gjilan because it was totally different from where I had been such as the Farmer's market in Halifax, Canada. There were so many goods such as food, clothes and electronics. What I was interested in most were the Albanian traditional clothes because they looked so gorgeous. My host sister explained to me which ones were for boys, girls, men and women. I wished I could have had a chance to wear the Albanian traditional clothing.

It was such a great opportunity that I could have a time to talk with some American Army soldiers who patrolled the city of Gjilan. What I asked was how they felt about staying in Kosovo. Since they were so nice and seemed not to mind spending their time with me, I could get a lot of interesting opinions from those who were trying to keep Kosovo safe.

Traveling around Kosovo with my classmates

It was such a memorable day to travel around Kosovo with my classmates. I truthfully enjoyed visiting the important historic sites and viewing nature.

Gadima

Since it was my first experience to visit a limestone cave, I was so excited to explore the inside of the cave. The inside of the cave was colder than I expected. It was a unique experience to see the various shapes of limestone. However, I could not see them in the way a guide explained them to me. For example, oval-shaped limestone looked like a pizza. Even though I could not get the ideas, it was impressive to see the beautiful limestone formations no matter how they looked. What depressed me about the limestone was when I touched it. It was not as beautiful as I had thought, but it was just wet and muddy. Since my hands got dirty, I washed them with cold water in a pond. It was so scary to use the water from the pond because it looked so deep that I could not see the bottom. In general, I had such a great time exploring the limestone cave although I did not have enough time to take a lot of pictures of the amazing limestone. If I had got lost, I thought I would have not been able to get out from the limestone cave.

Drenica

It was a great experience to visit Drenica because actually looking at what happened during the war was more impactful to my heart than hearing the stories of the war. I lost my words when I saw the Jashari house in Drenica. It was completely destroyed by considerable bullets and was set on fire after the massacre. I had not seen any damaged houses like the Jashari house before: It was painful to see the damaged house. However, what was more painful for me was to see the fact that there were some scribbles on the walls and garbage in the house. When I saw the Albanian flag hanging in the Jashari house, I received some messages appealing to my heart. I did not want to see something disrespectful to the Jashari house like that garbage and graffiti. What I thought was that it would be meaningful to get information about the story of the Jashari family and the war while looking at what happened during the war.

Rugova

I was lucky that I got a special lunch at a restaurant on the way to the Rugova Gorge. While I was waiting for what I ordered, I was talking to one of the clerks at the restaurant. After talking with him, he gave me additional beef, lettuce and tomato in my burger. In general, those who I met at restaurants in Kosovo were kind, nice and friendly to me.

It was one of my memorable experiences in Kosovo that I was having that great lunch while seeing the beautiful waterfall in Rugova. As I got close to the river, I thought the atmosphere was similar to what I had experienced in Japan. The reason why I felt so would be because the waterfalls were rocky, narrow and speedy. There was a great spot to view the river: it was on the edge of the manmade stone wall. I was relaxed rather than scared because the river view was amazing. What I was interested most in was the changing colour of the water in the river. For example, it looked colourless and clear where the river was shallow. In contrast, it looked light green where the river was deep.

Prizren

My favourite part of this travel was when I was visiting the city of Prizren. I enjoyed having a cup of macchiato while watching the river. What I liked most was the circumstance in the city of Prizren. It was the time for sunset when I was visiting Prizren. The orange sky made the city view of Prizren more beautiful. I enjoyed sitting on a bench near the river, which made me feel relaxed. What I was impressed with was the mosque. Green light was emitted from the top of the mosque when it got dark. There was one memorable experience in Prizren: I ate Red Bull flavour ice cream. Since I had never seen any ice cream with Red Bull flavour, I was so excited to eat it. The taste was not bad, but not as surprising as I expected.

I had fun learning some Albanian words such as "I love you" and "Will you marry me?" on the way back home. I found it interesting to learn how to speak Albanian because I liked the sounds of Albanian language. I thought it would be such a unique characteristic if I became able to speak Albanian because

I have never met anyone who spoke Japanese, English and Albanian.

Barbeque Party

I was really excited when I was invited for a barbeque party at one of classmates' house because he told me that there were swimming pools. Since it was great sunny day, I really wanted to go swimming. However, I did not feel like swimming in the swimming pools when I saw the colour of the water in the swimming pool. As the weather was getting nicer and nicer, I could not stand without going swimming. Once I jumped into the swimming pool, it was not as bad as I expected rather was good.

After swimming in the pool, I was so hungry and was impressed when I saw my classmates cooking Flija. Since I could not wait for it to be ready, I wanted to help them. What I did was to add additional milk on the Flija every five minutes. When I was waiting, I thought it was such a time-consuming work to cook Flija. The good thing was that the taste of the Flija was great so that it was worth being patient until the Flija got ready. Since I had many pieces of the Flija, I could not eat as much meat as I wanted to: I should have saved some space in my stomach for the meat.

It was such a fantastic experience to barbeque with my classmates. I appreciated those who bought the ingredients and cooked the great meal.

Bowling:

I truthfully enjoyed bowling and playing pool with my classmates at an amusement place for the last night of my stay in Kosovo. What I enjoyed most was playing pool because some of them were really good at it. Since I wanted to improve my pool skills, I asked them to teach me how to play pool well. It was great to get so much advice from those who were masters at playing pool. I will never forget the fact that I had so much fun with them that night.

My last day in Kosovo was same as I had spent for the last three weeks, except saying goodbye to my sweet friends. To be honest, I was not really sad saying goodbye because I somehow thought I would meet them again at some point in the future. It was true that I felt sad, but excitement to see them again was greater. I would like to go back to Kosovo to meet with my host family and those who I met in this program such as the great staff and my classmates. From the beginning to the end of this program, I was supported by wonderful people all around me. I was so happy that my older host brother, sister and their cousin came to Prishtina Airport to see me off. I cannot wait to see them again!

Due to my experiences throughout this program, my summer in 2012 became awesome.

Once I came back to Canada after my summer vacation in Japan, I have met some of those who I met in this program such as my classmates from Halifax, my professor and the television director. It was great to meet them again. I felt extremely happy. Once I saw their faces, I really felt like going back to Kosovo again. I look forward to meeting my sweet friends from Kosovo.

It was such a great experience to stay in the Balkan countries while participating in this program. It was one of the best and smartest decisions I have ever made to take an opportunity to be involved in this program. I really enjoyed what I had done, such as working out at a gym, travelling around the Balkan countries and communicating with those who I met in this program. Throughout this program, I learned so many things that have made my life more enjoyable. I would like to keep in touch with those who I met in this program.

I would like to mention my appreciation to those who gave and supported me to have such great experiences.

References:

Republika E Kosoves, 2012. On his first day of the official visit to Japan, Prime Minister Thaçi met the President of Japan External Trade Organization. Available from: http://www.mfa-ks.net/?page=2,4,1286

QUOTES

From the Balkans Peace Program 2012

"I thank you professor Bislimi and your foundation for the excellent job you're doing in educating young people and in building cultural, academic, and societal bridges between the young people of Kosova and their peers abroad."

Atifete Jahjaga
President of Kosovo

"The program was comprehensive in that there was an academic aspect, time for socializing and connecting with local people, official government visits, and the opportunity to visit various sites in Kosova and some of the surrounding countries. It would very difficult to experience the best of Kosova any other way. Kosova is a beautiful and fascinating place, rich in natural wonders, culture, history, and hospitality. I would go back in heartbeat."

Jessica Alexander
Participant, Balkans Peace Program 2012

"There is no better way to build the true image of Kosova and our people than by bringing here young scholars such as these students on your summer program. This is an educational program that helps the world better understand us and that helps us better see the world."

Jakup Krasniqi
Speaker of the Parliament of Kosovo

"My time in Kosovo on the BPP 2012 has put me on a different trajectory as an educator of adolescents: I am now driven to discuss grief, conflict, communication, and reconciliation whenever possible with my students."

Gordon MacKinnon
Participant, Balkans Peace Program 2012

"Our city has been privileged to have been the host of this program. TBG Foundation has continuously brought honour and shine to our city, our community and our country, through its educational programs. I am sure Gjilan has now become a new home away from home for the foreign students in this summer program."

Qemajl Mustafa
Mayor of Gjilan

"Overall, it was fortunate for me to learn an interesting topic like post-conflict developments with the great professor who kept me interested in the topic and my classmates who all are kind, friendly and funny. At the same time, it was also lucky for me that I could have shared a lot of wonderful experiences with them, I believe."

Masayuki Kishimoto
Participant, Balkans Peace Program 2012

"This program is one excellent way in which we can show the world what Kosova and the region have to offer and what we have learned from the past. I see this as a great way in which public diplomacy can work. These foreign students can be our best ambassadors throughout the world."

Ibrahim Gashi
Deputy Minister of Foreign Affairs
Government of Kosovo

"I am sure that nothing comes close to learning than the experience itself. Coming on this program, I am confident, will turn out to be a worthwhile endeavour for these students. What they learn here in a very short time is what they will probably remember for a long time."

Hajdin Abazi
Deputy Minister of Culture, Youth, and Sports
Government of Kosovo

ABOUT CONTRIBUTORS

Faton Tony Bislimi is a doctoral student of political science, specializing in comparative politics and international relations at the University of Alberta in Edmonton, AB, Canada. Prior to joining the University of Alberta, Tony was a doctoral fellow at the Centre for Foreign Policy Studies and EU Centre of Excellence, Department of Political Science, Dalhousie University in Halifax, NS, Canada. While in Halifax, Tony taught economics courses at both Dalhousie and Mount Saint Vincent Universities. He is president and founder of the Bislimi Group Foundation. Tony also holds an MSc in international development from Harvard University (2007), MA in international relations from Dalhousie University (2010) and honours BSc/BA in computer science/mathematics from Texas Lutheran University (2005).

Masayuki Kishimoto is a student of business administration at Mount Saint Vincent University in Halifax, NS, Canada. He is originally from Kyoto, Japan.

Laura Lussier is a student of political science and international development studies at McGill University in Montreal, QC, Canada. She enjoys sports, especially soccer, and is a devoted volunteer.

Gordon MacKinnon holds a Master's of Education degree from Mount Saint Vincent University in Halifax, NS, Canada. He also holds a BA in Education from the University of Ottawa and a BS in biology and history from Mount Allison University in Sackville, NB, Canada. Gordon has travelled and taught internationally in countries such as Colombia, Cuba, South Korea, etc.